the Sexy
Bitch's Party

the Sexy Bitch's Party

Living It, Throwing It & Being It

LULU DAVIDSON

Ulysses Press

Published in the United States by
Ulysses Press
P.O. Box 3440
Berkeley, CA 94703
www.ulyssespress.com

ISBN 1-56975-474-8
Library of Congress Control Number: 2005922421

Printed in Canada by Transcontinental Printing

1 3 5 7 9 8 6 4 2

Editor: Ashley Chase
Copy Editor: Sonya Nikadie
Production: Steven Zah Schwartz, Matt Orendorff
Cover artwork: gettyimages.com

Distributed in the U.S.A. by Publishers Group West

contents

introduction

So what is a sexy bitch? Sorry babe, there is no exact definition here to help you hone right in on this phenomenon. Instead, picture some sexy, confident women you know who get what they want and don't take no for an answer. They're creative and fun and they stand up for their beliefs. That's what a sexy bitch is. You may be picturing your grandmother, your boss, a girl you admired in high school, or a woman you see every day waiting for the bus. To be a sexy bitch there are no age, hair color, salary, or weight requirements. Instead, being a sexy bitch is about confidence, a willingness to take calculated risks, and a fondness for good times. Party womanimals appear to be endangered species, so it's time for us to start saving ourselves.

Partying is more than merely tossing back cosmos at the new club down the street. Women who love to party are open to finding good times wherever and whenever they arise, and these women are always attractive to others, because they are not afraid to flout conventional patterns of boring behavior. So lose the glass of "been there, seen that" merlot and scare up a colorful drink that requires a spiffy glass and has an intriguing name, preferably with sexual innuendo. Of course, you may decide not to lean in and coyly ask for a "sex on the beach" from Uncle Randy who is bartending your grandmother's 80th birthday party, but you get the basic idea for unleashing your wild woman ways when the time is right.

Not only will this book revitalize your partying attitude, but it also provides ideas for hosting your own parties. I know what you're thinking: planning, cleaning, and cooking. In today's age of Martha Stewart, being a hostess can cause an enormous amount of pressure. But look at where Martha's turbo hostessing landed her: she cracked and had to spend a six-month siesta in prison teaching origami techniques to crackheads! Surely you don't want this to happen to you! And really, who has time to make countless ramekins of crème brûlée from scratch? I certainly don't—and neither do most of the women I know.

If you relish rolling out tiny pie crusts and stuffing them to make millions of mini quiches, this is not the book for you. Instead, you can learn the secrets to stirring it up and hosting the low maintenance way, turning your place into the hottest one in town. Toss the mini quiches, go invest in a mini skirt, pull out your calendar, and let's get busy planning some good times.

Okay, now you're ready to dust off your silver go-go boots and make "Girls Just Wanna Have Fun" your cell phone ring, but I'd be remiss to not emphasize the importance of safety before we let the festivities begin. It is always wise to have a system arranged with a group of sexy bitches for knowing where each other are when your posse is out having a good time. Also, if you're out on a city street or in a cab alone, it's not a bad idea to pretend you are talking on your cell phone with someone while you are really staying alert about your surroundings; nefarious types will be less likely to mess with someone who they think is connected. Furthermore, know how much you can drink and when to stop. Being able to remember the previous evening's good times is always a good thing.

All of the ideas in this book have been tried out and all of the recipes have been tasted and applauded by women who don't host television shows and have magazines named after them—real women who are balancing hectic schedules with great times. This book is intended to give you fresh ideas for spicing up your social life (or jumpstarting it). The key is to believe that you are the most happening thing around. You can start the mantra now: I am a sexy bitch who loves to have fun!

part one:
being the party

Merely having some dancing shoes and a fully-stocked bar does not ensure your reputation as a party maven: you must also have the party persona. Ignore that nagging little voice urging you to bail on tonight's happy hour so that you will be rested for tomorrow's important client meeting; toss away your to-do list that is 897 items long; cast off your concerns about global warming and political events! Simply agree with me that forgoing an evening out on the town because of budget constraints, a bad hair day, or lack of a chic wardrobe is unacceptable. You were born to party and you must live the partying life. After all, there are plenty of exciting things to do that don't require wads of cash, and where there is a will to party there is a way to party.

So if you find yourself daydreaming at work about which Prada handbag to buy to accent the delicious new fur collar coat that you are planning on wearing to your friend's dinner party this weekend, do not berate yourself. Instead, welcome the bliss that accompanies having a packed social calendar and decide to go with the grayish blue leather bag. Clutch size. Silver accents.

The first way to embrace your inner party animal is to create a party persona. Sure, you can have a sexy alias (always a good thing to have ready), but what you really need is attitude. If you know how to sniff out a good time when you sense one nearby, you are on your way to a busy and enviable social calendar. What this means in a practical sense is that you need to communicate that you are a partyer who is not to be trifled with.

1 send the vibe that you're not afraid to dance on the bar

Blah, blah, blah, the television and newspapers are filled with bad news about everything these days and way too many people are succumbing to this contagious pessimism. A night out with the girls can easily be turned into an evening of complaining about the surplus of calories in everything that tastes good, micromanaging mothers, the exorbitant cost of living in America's coolest cities, and a million other depressing topics. Do NOT fall into this trap. Consider it your job to rise above worrying about bills, bosses, and bikini waxes and other things that can easily cramp a woman's fun-loving style. Be a trail blazer to sexy bitches everywhere and show them that it's okay to embrace hedonism for a change. What can you do to send the message that you love to have fun? Stick with these three golden rules to ensure that good times follow you wherever you are.

rule # 1: you're wearing fabulous shoes...don't keep them on the ground!!!

Why do we spend so much time and money expanding our shoe collection only to keep them hidden under tables and desks? Next time you feel like dancing, jump onto the highest structure—a table, bar, top of a car—and dance! (Note: If a car becomes your dance floor, just make sure it's not a soft-top. And make sure it's yours, or you might end up in an unseemly brawl with some auto nut whose paint job you just dinged.) That's right, move you and your fabulous shoes onto an improvised stage and show everyone what it really means to kick up your heels!

rule #2: meet new people

Yes, you have fabulous friends, but it's okay to branch out. Why are women surprised that they're never meeting new people when they go out with a group of other women who stick to each other like static cling? You're never going to meet anyone if you're constantly surrounded by people that you know. When you're out, socialize with bartenders, waiters, cab drivers, bouncers, and other partyers and see where it leads. You may learn about some fantastic party insider's tips if you open yourself up to other people around you. And who knows what that conversation with the cute bartender could lead to...at least maybe a free drink or two.

rule #3: be flexible

There is absolutely no reason to script out the entire evening's plan down to the minute. If you show up at a watering hole and it's just not happening, don't stay. Even if you've made plans to meet other people there, change the plan—that's what cell phones are for. If you hear about an interesting party, go check it out. In the journey that is the party life, often it is the unplanned stops along the way that are the most interesting.

2 make the right moves

To earn your sexy bitch black belt, you must master a few required moves. As the life of the party you must know how to make an entrance, work a room, flirt outrageously, and leave the other partyers wanting more when you leave.

exciting entrances

Before you enter any social gathering, take a deep breath and do a quick THANC check. What's this? Well, I'm about to spell it out for you...

T *teeth:* check your teeth for leftovers and lipstick streaks

H *hair:* avoid resembling Alfalfa

A *ass:* make sure you didn't sit in anything

N *nose:* are you sporting any boogers?

C *cleavage:* no boobs hanging out, please (or if you want them hanging out that's your biz)

It may seem overcautious, but you will thank me later for the THANC check. There is nothing worse than talking to the man of your dreams and having him point out that your front tooth is covered by a big black scrap of the olive you just popped into your mouth. (Okay, one thing is worse: he doesn't say anything and you discover it yourself minutes later.)

Once you have double-checked that you look fabulous, it is time to stand up straight and walk in with confidence. Scan the room for familiar faces and hot possibilities, but make your way to the bar before you descend on anyone so that you leave your options open and get a good layout of the scene. If anyone tries to waylay you, stay on course; no one wants to spend too much time at a party without having gotten a good look at it first.

Aside from making sure that you're not sporting any of the embarrassing problems previously mentioned, it's imperative that your arrival is known when you arrive at any social gathering. No, you don't need a trumpet player announcing your entrance, but you do want people to realize that you are a VIP (Very Important Partyer).

Have your theme song played as soon as possible when you arrive somewhere. Yes, you are a woman with a theme song, so you'd better pick one out if you don't have one already. Choose a song that you and your friends know well and can instantly start singing and dancing to as a way of picking up a party. And choose something that goes along with your image, so that when people hear the song they'll think of you. Consider a few of the following possibilities for theme song inspiration: "Dancing Queen" by Abba, "Love Don't Cost a Thing" by J. Lo, "Simply the Best" by Tina Turner, "Get the Party Started" by Pink, "I'm a Survivor" by Destiny's Child, "Just a Girl" by No Doubt, "I Feel the Earth Move" by Carol King, "Isn't She Lovely?" by Stevie Wonder, or "Hit Me with Your Best Shot" by Pat Benatar.

Be bold with your fashion statements. Since you're party royalty, you may as well be explicit about it: wear a crown or tiara. No one messes with a queen and that's what you are. You can make the look complete by sporting a sparkly boa as well or wearing a fabulous wig. This ensemble shows that you are confident and have a good sense of humor. When people ask if you're wearing all of this for a special occasion, simply shrug your shoulders and answer that every party is a special occasion.

Show up with an icebreaker—anything from a dart board or other game to a tray of cupcakes or jelly shots for handing out. Consider your icebreaker as a prop that you will use to start up conversation and attract people to you. A friend of mine went to a party with a life-sized promotional poster cut-out of Salma Hayek that she got from a local video store, and she introduced Salma to everyone as her best friend. Bizarre? Yes, obviously, yet she attracted all the men in the party to her as instantaneously as if she were Salma Hayek herself.

Make your entrance with pizzazz. Along with your fabulous crown and boa, rocking theme song, and icebreaker, it doesn't hurt to send the message that you're a firecracker. Literally. Show up with sparklers if it's the Fourth of July, Christmas crackers if it's Christmas, or noisemakers on New Year's Eve. Those ravey plastic glow-in-the-dark necklaces and bangles are good for any occasion. Find a way to announce that a sexy bitch is in the house.

shake it: working a room

As you work the room and mingle with as many people as possible, it's important to have a way of gauging romantic possibilities. Aside from obvious appearances, there are a few more subtle means of ascertaining a man's possibilities.

With so many men out there, it is important that you learn to identify the subtleties of what a handshake truly indicates so that you can winnow out the duds and start focusing on the dudes. True, not everyone shakes hands anymore, so you need to initiate the move if he doesn't. Waves and head nods do not cut it; you need some tangible evidence of how a man is going to feel up close. There is no faster litmus test for gauging a man than his handshake. Actually, this goes both ways, so make sure you don't shake hands wimpily yourself.

The first thing you want to look for should come as no surprise: a firm handshake. If his arm and hand wiggles like a wet noodle, there's a good chance that the rest of him isn't hard either. The second thing you want to look for is calluses along the top of the palm. You need to be careful here because an overly-calloused hand may indi-

LAME MAN WARNING SIGNS

- A Large Belt Buckle: If a man is wearing an overly large belt buckle, it could be that he is trying to overcompensate for something lackluster in the groin region. A large belt buckle is often a sign of insecurity and its wearer is best avoided.
- Too Much Hair Product: If a man is wearing more hair product than you are, avoid him at all costs. Enough said.
- Photo Wallet: If a man pulls out his wallet and begins to show you photos of his friends and family…or even worse, himself, it is time to find a new group with which to mingle.
- Pinky Rings: Ugh! It has been scientifically proven that men who wear pinky rings also tend to have extraordinarily hairy backs. As soon as you see this telltale sign of doom, back away (yes, pun intended).

cate that this guy is all brawn and no brains. (But make sure you get his number because he may come in handy on a moving day or something.) On the other hand, a thin line of calluses can indicate that he knows his way around a tool box and perhaps lifts weights, and this is clearly a promising sign of delightful things to come. The last key item to confirm is that he has buttery palms that are smooth but firm to the touch. Mmmmm.

If all indicators are that this guy has hands that are firm enough to wrestle up a good sweat yet tender enough to tempt you to investigate the rest of him, it's a green light. Go!

the not-so-subtle art of flirting

There are so many possibilities here that this section alone could merit its own book! Still, there are a couple of classic moves every sexy bitch should master so that she can own the men at every party.

the hair toss

Skip this paragraph if you are sporting a pixie do. Remember the scene in *St. Elmo's Fire* when Demi Moore executes the big hair toss? Sure you do. (Or if you don't, steer yourself to your local movie rental joint and get a reminder.) Now it's time for you to practice that same move so that you too can have the fellows wrapped around your little toe ring. Simply make sure that your luxurious tresses are in front of one of your shoulders. As you laugh at someone or something, take your freshly manicured hand and sassily flip your hair behind your shoulder. It doesn't sound like much, but with the right exposure of your gorgeous neck and your hair sparkling in the disco lights, the man of your choice is sure to be yours.

the nudge

Usually parties are crowded, right? Usually this is considered annoying, right again? Turn this inconvenience into an asset. Once you've spied the man who intrigues you most, walk by and slip sideways as you near him (because you must slither through the crowd) and brush against him. Will you turn away from him, brushing him with your rock-hard butt? Or brush him with your cleavage? Your choice. Make the gesture ambiguous enough so that he will wonder whether it was intentional or accidental. It's guaranteed that he will not leave your side for the rest of the evening.

the freudian slip

Ahhh, yes, one of the more interesting moves in the book, and also one of the most advanced. This must be executed flawlessly for sure-fire success. If you are someone who tends to giggle uncontrollably or flub your words, this move is not for you. The idea here is to slip a suggestive phrase or word into conversation with a hottie of your choice. You will leave him wondering: is he hearing voices, or living out one of his wildest fantasies?

what kind of dancer are you? (and I mean that in a nice way, really)

It's easy to play safe and avoid calling any sort of attention to yourself by meekly rocking from side to side on a crowded dance floor, but this will not send you into the partying history books. The key is letting go of your inhibitions, putting some shizzle into every move you make, and looking confident. Pick a style and go all-out.

spacey raver

When you close your eyes, you can see the music in dayglo colors swirling around your head, where you try to catch them with your waving arms. Or is that just a flashback? If your wandering hands "accidentally" swat some taut backsides, bonus!

disco holdover

Every Saturday night, you get the fever...

latina lover

You've found your inner J.Lo! Salsa, mambo, conga—you've got some of the sexiest moves on the dance floor.

swanky swinger

You and your "friend" know all kinds of fun old-fashioned steps, and aren't afraid to clear the floor with a well-placed dip and twirl.

two-steppin' cowgirl

The dance floor is your prairie, and you're rounding up the bulls.

team player

You like to combine forces with your friends and execute synchronized moves together, like Olympic swimmers but without the strange makeup and nose plugs. It doesn't really matter what you do—anything is fun when multiplied.

sexy swayer

Even if you would look ridiculous just trying to clap to the music, let alone dance in time, that's no reason to stay off the dance floor.

Dancing is the perfect excuse to sway your assets around and strike sexy poses. Just relax, and no one will notice you're rhythm-impaired.

funky breaking popper

You know all the latest steps, and incorporate them into a style all your own. Show off your fabulous skills—you don't need any advice from me!

If you're pulling your best moves on the dance floor but you still resemble a dying jitterbug, make some room and link up with some friends. Similarly, if you are stuck dancing with a guy with three or four left feet, you need to evacuate immediately. In either case, start to groove with your gal pals. Strength in numbers will camouflage your dancing problems while simultaneously playing right into every guy's fantasy of a little gal-on-gal action. *So* hot—and problem solved.

intriguing exits

As always, keep them wanting more. Make sure that you do not corner people and yammer on all about you. When you sense conversation dwindling, do not attempt to resuscitate. Instead, bow out of languishing chit chat with "Hmm, I think I'm going to check out the food," or "My drink needs a refill, can I get you something?" or the old standby, "I'm going to powder my nose." After all, the days of bladder buster parties (drinks are free until someone uses the loo) have hopefully vanished after your college years.

If you're exchanging numbers with a fine find, make sure you give out your real number—or at least an email address. If someone of the not-so-fine category asks for your digits, be sure to have a fake number on hand that does not begin with 555. Try to make it close to your real number so if you should ever happen to run into this person again, you can blame the missed connection on a minor error; this way everyone saves face.

When your inner party-o-meter tells you that this event is played out (food and drink levels are getting precariously low, music is sounding strained, and people are acting itchy), it's time to get out of the joint. Round up your posse and plan the next stop on your party circuit. Start spreading the word that the queen is moving and everyone who is anyone better get involved with your exit strategy. Once you have rounded up a sizeable herd, it's time to leave the party. You entered with a theme song; why not leave on a high note with a signature goodbye song? Have them crank out Madonna's version of "Don't Cry for Me Argentina" to set the right tone—play your cards right, and everyone may end up raising their lighters in tribute to your party persona.

And of course, on your way out, be sure to toss out a "thank you, love you, miss you, mean it" to the host.

3 look like a party waiting to happen

Okay, being a sexy bitch is all about attitude and confidence—not what you look like. Still, it's fun to dress the part. You'd never go into space without a space suit, so unless this weekend's birthday party is the kind you can attend in your birthday suit, make sure you wear your party dress (or party jeans, or party whatever). Think of your wardrobe as your party armor: wear anything that makes you feel ready to conquer the world.

beauty and the party beast

I'm not going to tell you to work out six days a week and to get 10 hours of sleep at night, because this is unrealistic for most busy women (especially sexy bitches with a social life), but I do encourage you to have some sort of beauty regimen, even if it merely includes washing your face and brushing your teeth after a late night. Create some standards and stick with them. True sexy bitches figure out a way to combine working out with getting out and shaking it. Go walking with some friends, go out dancing. And of course, there's also a sexy romp with your partner to burn a few calories.

Sexy bitches may forgo nights of sleep because they are out all night partying or perhaps they are enjoying a private one-on-one type of party that precludes sleep, but they know to catch up on beauty sleep when they get the chance. The best way to fend off a case of the party poopers is to ensure you are adequately recharging your batteries when you need to. So don't be afraid to nap. Even if it's a gorgeous day outside and the rest of the world appears to be outside enjoying it. Instead, take solace in the luxury of cuddling up and relaxing. You deserve it and need it.

to roar, you need a great mane

Situation: You want to color your hair with the adorable caramel streaks that appear to be crowning the manes of the world's top models, but you must also pay this month's rent.

Options:

A. Keep your hair *au naturel* and learn to love it. Those "top models" are all skanks, anyway.

B. Go to the drugstore and buy a do-it-yourself highlighter kit. Okay, so this isn't a bad option because those kits keep getting better and better, but there can be a few minor problems. For one thing, you can only see part of your head and so you may end up with a really lopsided job. If you get a friend to help you, make sure that she has not been drinking or you may end up resembling a tie-dyed T-shirt.

C. Damn your budget and go treat yourself to the salon. How do you rationalize this? Easy. It has been proven in countless studies (and all of those corny candid camera shows) that good-looking people get promoted more often than plain Janes. Therefore, since job security is essential to ensuring that you will be able to cover you rent over the long-term, you should definitely go for the dream 'do. Consider it an unemployment insurance payment.

Do not torture yourself with bad hair days if you know a trip to the salon can take care of this. Never feel guilty about spending money on maintaining a marvelous mane. Hair is your important accessory, so don't skimp and use those dreadful spray bottles that lighten your hair in the sun or with the use of a hairdryer unless you're trying to look like a scarecrow. The flip side of this is not to skimp on hair removal. Sure, it's easier and cheaper to shave your bikini line, but who wants to look like they have a case of pubic pox? Opt for the bikini wax and remember that they hurt less and less the more you get them.

farther down

Speaking of ignoring pain, always wear the most impressive heels you can find. In your closet, you should have a wide array of different options for your feet, including colors other than black. Yeah, everyone knows that high heels are bad for your back, but if you have a few cocktails the pain in your back and feet always goes away. Oh, and don't date a chiropractor or you will never hear the end of it.

Another strategy to maximizing your beauty and sexy factor is to focus on one key accessory. After all, men are fairly simpleminded and can become overwhelmed with too much sensory stimulation, so go for a "shock and awe" effect with a dramatic piece of jewelry, a suede or leather jacket, or a soft and strokeable sweater or tank top. Remember: men like bright and shiny objects.

Supposedly skin is out, and I'm waiting for this message to trickle down to the masses. It seems there is too much jiggle and butt cleavage all over the place, and there's nothing sexy about thongs hanging out for the world to see unless you're the 0.01 percent of the population lacking a single ounce of cellulite. For the rest of us, keep it all tucked in and maintain a sense of dignity. If you're planning on showing skin, always opt for cleavage.

what's in your closet?

Three black skirts are not enough! (For one thing, going topless in public can get you arrested in some states.) Not having just the right outfit is enough to put any girl out of the partying mood, so it's key to have all of the essential basics for hitting the town.

sexy bitch black pants

One of my missions in life is to locate the perfect pair of black pants. Okay so it's not as noble as discovering the cure for a disease, but it's a goal nevertheless. Anyway, I'm still looking. You want to find a pair that is formal, yet casual enough to wear out and not worry about. They should look great with boots and heels. Black pants are a fundamental building block to any sexy bitch's wardrobe because they should flatter your figure and go with everything.

a perfect black skirt

You pick the length and style: mini, A-line, long, whatever. The point is to have a basic skirt that makes your legs, hips, and ass look terrific. You should be able to wear this out for a dinner date or out dancing with no problem.

a distinctly fashionable jacket

Once again, you pick the texture and style: pea coat, denim, suede, who cares? What you're trying to accomplish here is having a jacket that is an accessory that is going to win you compliments and make you stand out amongst a dreary crowd of black trench coats. Find a jacket that has a distinctive cut, patterned fabric, or interesting edging. Don't worry about finding a classic coat that will last you for the next five winters. Instead, sink some cash into a gem of a jacket that will catch people's eye today.

a sparkly top

Find a cut that suits your figure and find some outlandishly fun tank top or T-shirt that will make you noticed. V-necks tend to be flattering on everyone and make cleavage, small and voluptuous alike, look fabulous. Find a top with great, interesting texture that invites touching. Do not limit yourself to black but consider picking a fun color that sticks out and says, "Out of my way; sexy bitch in the house."

mean jeans

Every sexy bitch needs a pair of jeans that can be worn to either a baseball game or the swanky new café that opened downtown. Over the last few years, jeans have become *de rigueur* for any gal with style.

While some people shy away from jeans because they think they're unflattering, that's ridiculous. There are so many styles now that you can spend a whole weekend trying on millions of pair without replicating the same style twice. Jeans come in many different colors now too, and all are terrific. I'd lean toward a darker pair; they will likely be a little more versatile for dressier events. Find a pair that is soft enough to feel comfy in but that shows off your delicious bod.

a dress that screams sexy bitch

Any boring what-to-wear book will emphasize the importance of the versatile black cocktail dress, so I'm going to skip it and tell you to snag something sexy that is not black. That's right, ditch the black dress in favor of something shimmery and unique. Look for a dress with a nifty neckline or plunging back. Go for something unique and memorable and think color or silver. You want to be noticed for your style, not your ability to blend into the crowd, so move out to the center of the room in your va-va-va-voom silver flapper dress and leave all the gals in their boring classic black cocktail dresses and pearls in the corner. Consider pairing your dress with knee-high boots or even cowboy boots to change it up a little. Make sure you dress is flexible enough to dance in and don't be afraid to sport some cleavage. If you don't have much in this department, tape your breasts together to add some drama to the décolletage.

what to wear underneath

The intriguing little items you might be wearing underneath your fabulous ensemble are just as important as what is clearly visible to the masses. Consider it safe to always assume that you will end up wearing only your underwear at some point in the evening. You don't want to be stuck in your granny hip hugger flowered underpants (note: none of us ever admit to owning those—ever), do you? I didn't think so.

Don't skimp on skimpy bras and panties—invest in them the way you invest in the rest of your wardrobe. And don't feel limited to black, white, and cream when it comes to lingerie shopping. Avoid buying those dreaded pantyhose (ugh!) and opt for the thigh-highs instead. They are much more comfortable, and you can mix-and-match them if they run instead of buying a whole new pair. Plus, they look much hotter when you're baring down than a body wrapped from bellybutton to toe in spandex.

accessorize, accessorize, accessorize!

You can have the greatest clothes in the world, but what's the point if you don't add a little sparkle here and there? Jewelry is every sexy bitch's best friend. Earrings, necklaces, bracelets, rings, and don't forget the all-important toe ring. You are not trying to resemble Liberace, but adding some jangle and bling is essential to crafting a unique and stylish look. Other opportunities to dazzle include shoes, belts, hats, and handbags. Okay, so not everyone was born to sport a hat, but check a few out and see if anything works for you.

I confess to being addicted to buying shoes and bags—but really, there are worse vices. Once again, don't just buy black here. Go for color, texture, and shape, and mix them up. Contrary to the old rule our mothers taught us, your handbag and shoes do not need to be the exact same color. That's right, be wild and carry the lime green tote while gracing the world with your fuchsia beaded slippers: everyone will love your look.

the look on the go

Sexy bitches should always be ready to look luscious. If you're serious about getting your groove on, you need to be ready to go in a nanosecond. There are a couple of quick things you should do to revive your look after a long day at the office. Reinvigorate your hair, skin, and makeup.

One easy way to liven up a drooping do is to keep a clip in your purse and clip your hair up toward the end of your work day and spritz a little hairspray on your hair as you twist it up into a messy updo. If you plan in advance, you can even braid it loosely during the day to get those same tresses that earn Julia Roberts the big bucks. When the clock strikes quitting time, you can literally let your hair down and look tousled yet terrific. Incidentally, overly perfect hair can turn guys off because they'll think you won't want to mess it up—yet a stylishly shaggy mane says, "Shag me." Let your hair send the message that you could roll around anywhere, anytime.

Now that all of the major facial cleanser brands produce wipes, it would be absolutely irresponsible to ignore them. Freshen up that dazzling complexion of yours in no time with these little spa wipes. You will wake up that skin from a dulling day at the office and be ready to glow on the go. Also be ready to apply a little blush and mascara to liven up eyes that are fatigued from staring at a computer screen all day.

Other little toiletries to stash in your goodie bag include some ibuprofen, tampons, deodorant, a toothbrush, and toothpaste. Oh, there are also those fabulous spot removers that come in little envelopes to rescue your look in case you spill sangria on your cashmere tank top. All of the items can be found in sample sizes so there is no reason to carry around a bag that requires a sherpa. Include them in your purse or work bag because they come in handy at the office and will save you some grief if you spend the night unexpectedly somewhere other than your own pad.

4 party crisis management

Unfortunately every night can't be the best night of your life. We've all been stuck cornered by some annoying guy with sewer breath recounting the intricacies of his latest appointment with his proctologist, but don't let these low points discourage you and become a continual pain in your ass. Here are a few surefire ways to liven up a lame party.

party crisis #1

An event has landed on your social radar that requires a date, yet you really don't feel like leaving yourself stuck with one guy for the evening.

SOLUTION: Men are like accessories; they are best when they can be mixed and matched to the right situation. You wouldn't wear the same shoes to everything, so why are women expected to use the same man for everything? Forget it and go with the "male accessory plan." Every sexy bitch should have a selection of men that go best with certain occasions. Here is an outline of the type of men you want on hand for the different events that crop up in every sexy bitch's life.

gregarious greg

This is a charming, outgoing, and laid-back friend who is best brought to dinner parties hosted by other sexy bitch friends of yours. He's quick to laugh, has funny stories of his own, and is easy to leave unattended for lengths of time while you socialize with others. You two should have a friendly relationship that endures over time yet never really leads to anything hot and heavy that has the chance of becoming permanent. Easy on, easy off!

spendy spencer

This is the guy you call when you need to be pampered. Maybe your party fund is getting low but your appetite for partying is still on high and you need someone to supplement your income. You need Spendy Spencer on speed dial so that he can show up on a moment's notice to take you out for a tasty and *trés* chic dinner or a lavish night on the town. He's got his own *Zagat's Guide*, impeccable manners, and a fancy set of wheels, so he knows where the quality action is and how to get there in style. In the best case scenario, Spendy Spencer has an crush on you and thinks that you're a goddess who is beyond his reach (which you are) so he's always willing to rise to whatever you ask for without expecting huge returns.

sporty bob

If you feel like a hike or are itching for a surfing outing, Sporty Bob is the guy for you. His boyish charm and rugged good looks are enough to raise your adrenaline anytime for an athletic adventure. He may not own a single oxford shirt or a suit, but who needs those when you're looking for an endorphin rush? Incidentally, your excursions often end with a little private romp somewhere with a good night's sleep.

reckless rafe

When you're feeling wild, who you gonna call? Reckless Rafe. He's unpredictable, a seasoned partyer, and a man with an appetite for fast times. He likes to dance, so he's a great find for a night on the town. You may show up together at a club and each go home with someone else and there are no hard feelings (or at least any resentment fades after a week or two). Or you two may end up tanked enough for a wild hedonistic night together. He's like a human version of Vegas: sometimes you get lucky, sometimes you don't.

TOD (pronounced todd, but it's actually an acronym for touch of dork)

This is the guy you want around when you need to feel smart. Big office party coming up the week before your annual review? Bring TOD. He'll dazzle your boss with his flawless manners, conservative yet crisp sense of fashion, and mind-boggling range of knowledge on business and technology topics, plus he sports an alarmingly keen memory for all news stories. He's the kind of guy your mother would love for you to marry but, hey, you just don't just don't see yourself living with a white picket fence and 2.4 children.

tender tim

Looking for that sweet-hearted fellow who will join you for an art opening or documentary film viewing at your local alternative cinema? Try Tender Tim. He is very interested in cultural diversity, the environment, and free-range chickens. True, he can be annoying with his touching displays of compassion, but sometimes someone with a little bit of heart is needed to counteract you.

bitchy ben

This is the fellow who will join you for shopping and manicures, can dish about all of your favorite shows, sing all of the lyrics of every Britney Spears song, and successfully convince you that Cindy Crawford has fat ankles. He is gay so there is no chance that you two will hook up unless you're feeling very experimental.

party crisis #2

You arrive at a co-worker's party where there is no music and no food, and there seems to be a large contingency of nerds standing around debating the effectiveness of the leading brands of pocket protectors.

SOLUTION: Before you run to the door, study the scene for any hint of possibility. Don't forget that one of the all-time most famous party scenes takes place in *Revenge of the Nerds*. You are a professional partyer and this is your challenge. Do you have what it takes to have these guys swinging from the rafters? Repeat after me: yes, I am a sexy bitch and I will make this party happen. First of all, make these nerds believe that they are hot: flirt, canoodle, giggle, whatever it takes to turn on their pocket flashlights. Once these fellows feel confident and cut loose, the fun is going to fizz over like a long-corked bottle of champagne because these guys have been waiting for this moment of having a hot sexy bitch in their midst since they were little pimple-faced adolescents sneaking *TV Guide* cover shots of Heather

Locklear under their bedroom mattresses. Rock on and make their night. You are a goddess and they are your cabana boys.

party crisis #3

You are wearing your sexiest pair of pants, but they burst a seam or get a major stain and it looks like your night is over.

SOLUTION: Do not tie a sweater around your waist. I repeat: do not tie a sweater around your waist. This looks dreadful and will make your ass look enormous. You have a couple of options.

First, the conservative approach: take a more chic approach to this fashion catastrophe and tie a pashmina or shawl around your waist to give yourself a tapered appearance of skirt over pants. No one will even suspect there was a crisis.

Now, the real party girl approach: delight your fellow partyers with some innocent flashing. Hey, why not? You may even find that the flashing becomes contagious and you may single-handedly drive the event into an unscripted clothing optional party. Nicely played!

party crisis #4

You wake up with a stranger.

SOLUTION: Hopefully your first impression isn't that you need to call local pest control. Take a deep breath. Do you like what you see? Are you at your house or at some unknown location? If you're at your house, wake him up in a fluster and tell him that your strict mother is on her way over and that he'd better vamoose if he doesn't want to end up with a major scolding. If you're at his place, collect all of your goods and stealthily hit the high road. You can get your bearings outside.

If you've just rolled over and encountered a Jude Law look-a-like, tuck yourself back into bed and contemplate what he's going to make you for breakfast.

party crisis #5

All of the year's hottest social events fall on the same evening.

SOLUTION: What's up with everyone scheduling their blow-outs for the exact same night? Don't stress. Line them all up and get your fine self ready for a night of back-to-back action. If all the events call for a different level of formality, opt for a slinky number that can go either direction. Go for a hot tank top—perhaps a sequined halter top—and a denim skirt or sexy black pants. The great thing about dark denim is that it looks a little nicer and everyone is wearing it to everything. Be fearless and conquer all of the evening's events.

party crisis #6

Your friend becomes a belligerent drunk.

SOLUTION: We all know someone with a Dr. Jekyll/Mr. Hyde personality. As the evening begins they're charming and entertaining, but you would rather swim in a pool of piranhas than hang out with them after they've had a few drinks. If it's a girlfriend, she gets weepy, insecure, and argumentative; if it's a guy, he gets pissed off and wants to fight everyone. Great—either way they're bound to get you in trouble. So how do you manage this nightmare? I hate to say it, but ditch them. If this is a recurring pattern, why do you want to be friends with someone so volatile anyway?

party crisis #7

The party appears to have run out of gas.

SOLUTION: First of all, you may want to consider rounding up your posse and hitting the road. If you feel compelled to stay for some reason, there are a few strategies you can employ to resuscitate this par-tay:

- One crowd pleasing party game that is rarely broken out after middle school is Spin the Bottle. Sure, it's immature, but can you think of a better way to get people to loosen up than getting some kissing going around?
- Announce that a certain word is banned. Make it a commonly used word, such as "like" or "said." If someone says that word, they must pay for it with truth or dare: answer any question asked (make the questions as embarrassing as possible), or take the dare: have a shot, kiss the nearest person, take off one article of clothing, etc. See where things go from there…
- Everyone should speak in an accent of their choice. This is silly but it can be a good icebreaker if people are acting uptight.
- Start the "What if…" game. Ask people questions that are sure to elicit some controversy and zany brainstorming. Examples: What if you had to either burn or freeze to death; which would you choose? What if you could only eat one thing for the rest of your life; what would you eat? What if you were stranded on a deserted island; what are the three things you would want

with you? What if you were an Olympian; which sport would you compete in?

- Set up an obstacle course and make guests race it. This can be fun for a barbeque or outdoor party, but it also works indoors. Your course can include a

food station where someone must snarf something down, some hurdles, something to crawl through or under, a stint on roller skates, and other challenges. Time everyone and crown winners once everyone is tired out.

party crisis #8

You MISS A PARTY because you a) forgot, b) couldn't find the address in all the slips of paper floating around your purse, c) accidentally scheduled a vacation for the same weekend.

SOLUTION: As I'm sure you've guessed, this is the worst party crisis of all: any party can be saved as long as you're there, but if you miss it, all is lost.

The girl who has it all also needs to keep track of it all; this is where a planner comes in. If you're a techie type, by all means, indulge your inner nerd and sport the latest in PDA accoutrements, but I should point out that there is a reason why Kate Spade does not make electronic devices. Fine, carry one anyway.

If you're more of a creative type who enjoys doodling and experimenting with your signature, go out and buy yourself a fabulously stylish planner. Alligator skin, polka dots, whatever, just make certain that it sends the message that you love funky trinkets. Be sure there is a little pad of paper in it so that you can hand out your digits to desirable dates.

Of course everyone should carry a cell phone. This may seem inconsistent with my message about PDAs, but cell phones are a whole different story. First of all, they are actually a safety device and can be used to keep tabs on your precious posse. Second, they come in delicious colors and can accessorize even the blandest of outfits fetchingly. Lastly, you can take pictures with them and memorialize any moment. Fun!

5

party aftermath: hangover helpers

Ahhh, the most important topic you will need to survive the party circuit: how to live through hangovers. Hangovers are the worst, and they can range from mild dehydration and fatigue to full-out puking all day. Sometimes you wake up with them, sometimes they creep up on you later. If you have reason to believe that your hangover is dangerously dehydrating or you are uncontrollably ill, you should head to your nearest local hospital.

So what do you do if you're at work and hung over beyond belief? Hide out as best you can. Stick around your desk, duck behind your computer monitor, and keep your head buried in binders and reports so no one bugs you. If you must get up from your desk to use the photocopier or something, make sure you mumble about how busy you are the whole time and check you watch like you're feverishly up against a deadline. No one will bug you because they won't want to get roped into helping you and doing more work. When you have a free moment, run out and get some lunch from McDonald's or some other greasy spoon; it may provide a few minutes of much-needed relief. If your phone has an option that lets you turn the ringer off, silence that damn jingling so you won't be bugged by peevish clients or a micromanaging boss. Obviously, if you can work from home, do it.

I'm not going to lie; there is no one-size-fits-all cure for hangovers, but here's a compilation of some of the most tried-and-true remedies for getting you through that dreaded next day.

hangover helper #1: a shower

Sometimes getting up and cleaning off helps. A good shower can revive you and rinse the party grime away for another day, but sometimes showers can leave you hot, drained, and cranky. Even if a shower doesn't make you feel better, it can leave your muscles feeling like putty—which helps you crawl back into bed and get some more sleep. If you try the shower option, make sure that you have a cool drink somewhere in the bathroom to prevent you from getting overheated and more dehydrated.

hangover helper #2: a cold bottomless drink

Some people swear by following up a raucous evening with a chaser of beer or liquor in the morning, but I don't recommend it. What most of my friends prefer is iced coffee, ice tea, cola, ginger ale, or some other cold, carbonated drink. Water works for some, but it should be really icy to do the trick. Caffeinated drinks are good because they constrict blood vessels, helping prevent a major hangover headache.

hangover helper #3: cold air/water

Ski or beach vacations guarantee hangovers because you tend to overindulge after skiing or while draped on the beach. Fortunately a potential cure is within reach. If you can go swimming in some cool water, go for it. Nothing washes away a hangover like a refreshingly cold dip. One warning: avoid hot tubs or hot springs. I have a miserable memory of visiting a hot springs spa the day after my twenty-first birthday and wallowing in hot, smelly (I think it was a sulfur spring), dingy water and wishing desperately that I could leave.

Another important thing to note: if you're suffering from a hangover in a hot climate, avoid the sun and overly hot temperatures. Do not go out and bake in the sun or you will regret it. In addition, avoid any next-morning boat cruises (nothing jumpstarts a hangover quite like motion sickness) and do not go scuba diving, or you may find yourself feeding the fish with your vomit. Just go for an easy swim and then take a nap in the shade.

If you're in a colder climate, a ski run is just what you need. Yes, it may be brutal to stuff yourself into all of those hot layers of clothing and jam your equipment on, but you will be happy when the cold air hits your face. A few runs down an easy slope, and you'll be ready for that afternoon's happy hour. If the idea of hitting the slopes makes you feel so green that you know it's an impossibility, just get outside for a walk around the ski condo or to the end of the street. Breathing in some cold air will get you to slow down and may settle the hot queasy feeling that is nagging you.

hangover helper #4: vitamins

Some people swear by Vitamin C as a surefire way to beat a hangover. It's never really worked for me, but swill down some orange juice and see if it floats your boat. If the acidity of a citrus juice scares you, try a Vitamin C tablet. I've also heard about the wonders of Vitamin B-complex. Once again, this has never done it for me, but give it a shot. (Oops, sorry if the word "shot" is toxic to you right now.)

hangover helper #5: more sleep

This is my personal favorite. If there is any way that you can remain in bed or take a mid-morning nap, this is definitely the way to go. More often than not, a hangover is the remnant from a night of low quality sleep, so if you can get up, have something to eat, get outside briefly, and then go back for a nap, you will probably find yourself a happier camper.

hangover helper #6: eat what you want

When you're hung over, you may feel like you never want to see food again, or you may be ravenous and craving the greasiest meal you can get your hands on. Do not feel guilty about consuming 2,000 calories in one meal right off the bat; those weirdos who gobble down fruit and salads the next morning should be avoided at all costs. When you're hung over, you should throw out any diet obligations.

Most of us crave things like omelets, hash browns, French fries, pizza and Asian food. Usually saltier is better. And if someone else makes it for you, that's even better.

quiz: are you a bona fide sexy bitch?

Are you a partying sexy bitch or what??? Take the quiz and figure out if you need to return to the junior varsity squad.

1. What should every sexy bitch have in her handbag?
   - A. breath mints
   - B. fake eyelashes
   - C. cell phone
   - D. a stash of confetti

Answer: C. Okay, so I started out easy. Although there is no doubt that fake eyelashes and confetti can play key roles in spicing up any moment of the day, a cell phone is an absolute necessity for multiple reasons. It keeps you dialed in to all of the latest and greatest happenings, you can get directions to anywhere by calling information, and you can always use it to discourage unwanted conversation by pretending to hold a conversation with an imaginary someone on the other line. Breath mints are a close second, but can usually be picked up easily if the need arises.

2. If you had to celebrate one holiday every day for the rest of your life, what would it be?
   - A. Christmas
   - B. your birthday
   - C. St. Patrick's Day
   - D. Halloween

Answer: B. As tempting as it is to wear a Halloween costume all of the time, your birthday should be the obvious winner here. Everyone loves Christmas, but really why would you want to celebrate someone else's birthday?

3. Where is the worst place to party?

    A. a canoe

    B. stuck in traffic

    C. a chairlift

    D. a movie theater

Answer: A. Unfortunately I speak from experience with this one. It sounds fabulous to spend a day on the water basking in the sun, but I can verify that canoes are extremely tippy—and are much harder than you would think to right without getting tons of water inside. I'll bet that there are lots of lakes with sunken canoes littering the bottoms. If you don't want to lose your party spread (and your keys, etc.), stick to stable party staging areas.

4. Situation: A male cop shows up at your door when you're hosting a ladies night. He says he's received complaints that the party is too rowdy. What is the best way to greet him?

    A. Apologize and say you'll keep it down.

    B. Pretend there is no party.

    C. Invite him in and offer an appetizer plate.

    D. Assume he is a male stripper and commence to tear his uniform off wildly.

Answer: C. You can play this one safe and go with A (although playing it safe is not the sexy bitch way...) or you can be a little more coy and opt for B, but I recommend you give C a try, especially if the cop's a hot young thing who could conceivably be mistaken for a stripper. I don't recommend going all the way with option D, though, unless you want to experiment with turning the county lock-up into a party venue. If he's really a stripper, he'll let you know soon enough. In fact, it's a good idea in general to know who you're dealing with BEFORE you tear his pants off.

5. If you could create a holiday that memorializes an important historical moment in sexy bitch history, which would a true sexy bitch want?
    A. Invention of the Wonderbra Day
    B. Margaret Sanger Day
    C. Creation of the Office Cubicle Day
    D. Food on a Stick Day

Answer: A. While it's impossible to overstate the significance of such culinary developments as the lollipop, popsicle, and corndog, it's even more mindboggling to imagine life without the Wonderbra. It's important to remember that there was a time when some women were forced to feel inferior and less appreciated. Now sexy bitches everywhere can stand forward with their shoulders thrown back and celebrate the joy of a well-endowed bust without the physical inconveniences that can accompany such a figure (back aches, etc.) PS: B is a close second. In case you didn't know, Margaret Sanger was the original "Sex and the City" girl; this New Yorker published educational information about birth control back in the dark ages when it was illegal in America, and she even went to jail for her efforts. Now where would we be today without such tenacious historical sexy bitches?

6. When is it time to leave a party?

    A. When Vanilla Ice's Greatest Hits album is put on the sound system

    B. When you spot someone else wearing the same outfit as you are

    C. When the host goes to bed

    D. When someone breaks out Dungeons and Dragons

Answer: D. Why should you cut your evening short just because someone else dared to show up in YOUR outfit? Remember, you're the one who looks smashing in whatever you are wearing and everyone else looks like a mere impostor. Your cue to leave is when weird people start crawling out of the woodwork to play a lame game like Dungeons and Dragons. Now if it's Spin the Bottle instead, you should be in the front row…

7. What must every sexy bitch be associated with?

    A. A signature drink

    B. The must-have invitation

    C. A deadly wit

    D. All of the above

Answer: D. Duh! Must I say more?

8. What is the most critical sexy bitch accessory?

    A. the darling boy toy

    B. the boa

    C. the shoes

    D. the fluffy white dog that fits in your purse

Answer: C. All of these are delightful options to have on hand, but I think I'm going to have say that a fabulous pair of shoes can be like a secret weapon against party apathy everywhere. If you are going to splurge on anything, make it shoes. They can perk up even the dullest of days!

9. What is a great present for a sexy bitch?
   A. a spa gift certificate
   B. a packet of charming thank you cards
   C. theater tickets
   D. a cashmere sweater

Answer: A. Every sexy bitch needs her special time to be pampered and enjoy a relaxing mani/pedi or massage. Ahhhhh!

10. If you have to call in sick to work (when you really have a hangover), what is your best excuse?
   A. diarrhea
   B. eye problem
   C. strange highly contagious 24-hour skin fungus
   D. admit to the hangover

Answer: B. The truth may set you free, but it may set you free with a whole bunch of free time—because no boss wants to hear that her star employee is hung over. Go with "eye problem" instead. The beauty to this subtle masterpiece of an excuse is that no one will doubt you. If you show up the next day and your coworkers are curious about your "eye problem," simply tell them, "I couldn't see myself coming to work yesterday."

part two:
living the party life

The party life is the big leagues—it's a tough game, and some win the gold while others burn out and end up doing ads for used car dealerships. Don't let this happen to you! Professional athletes know how to read their playing field to complete passes, avoid interceptions, and score points. To be a party pro, you need to be able to read a party scene, identify obstacles, and capitalize on opportunities to score. Think of me as your gruff trainer with the heart of gold: I'm in your corner, ready to give tough love when you need it. Just don't spit in my bucket!

Challenges arise on this demanding life path, and sometimes life throws lemons. As a party goddess it is your job to make those lemons into lemon drop shots (sorry, but lemonade is just too tame for sexy bitches). I'll help you learn to thrive on minimal sleep, look spiffy in a jiffy, and throw a fabulous party in a second. To complete your sexy bitch arsenal of tricks, you need a selection of men to fit every whim and solutions to common party faux pas—you'll find it all in this section. (Well, not the actual men, but a guide to choosing them.) Now is the time to put your friends on speed dial and get this show on the road, unless you want to be left as roadkill on the party superhighway.

6 mundane events that call for more festivity

Any sexy bitch worth her salt knows that parties aren't something you go to; they are something you DO. So don't sit around like Cinderella waiting to be invited to the ball (unless you have a special connection to a fairy godmother); you've got to make this party happen here and now. Here's how to take the most boring, ordinary toad of a day and transform it into a prince of a party with your sweet kiss. (Watch that tongue!)

laundry night

If you are one of those lucky people without a washer and dryer in your home, getting your duds ready for the next party doesn't have to be lonely, boring housework: it can be a party in itself. Pack up a radio, whip up a pitcher full of cocktails, and hit the laundromat. If a hot guy happens to be there, make sure you leave your sexiest undergarments out for him to see, offer him a drink, and get ready to make a new friend.

moving day

Ugh, no one likes to deal with packing, unpacking, chasing down dust bunnies the size of Texas, hanging pictures, and all of the things that are required to move from one pad to another. So, if you have a moving day approaching you better liven things up and have a good time planned. First of all, hopefully you can line up some strapping lads for the heavy lifting and you'll need to make it worth their while (you can determine exactly how "worth it" you want to make this). Get some beers and order in some food for your helpers. Nothing is more necessary after a long day of hauling things around than a couple of cold ones. And when you arrive in the new place, you have the perfect excuse to throw a housewarming party.

picking someone up at the airport

If you have a friend or family member flying into town and they have a good sense of humor, greet them in the baggage area with a sign that says, "Welcome home from rehab." Or you could always carry a sign that says, "Camp Bare-Ass Nudist Reunion" and shout out that you almost didn't recognize them with their clothes on. This is a sure-fire way to start off a terrific weekend.

tax day

No one looks forward to April 15th, so why not be the person to turn it around and call together a soiree? You can hand out Monopoly money to your fellow partyers to make them feel like they're getting some moola back, while simply focusing everyone on relaxing your problems away with a few cocktails. If you get the vibe that everyone's feeling tight on cash, make sure that your night out happens at a Happy Hour with terrific deals. Or maybe someone is getting back a nice fat rebate and they want to treat everyone to a round. Who knows? It's up to you to make the party out of an otherwise lame day.

a friend has surgery

Your poor friend just had his/her tonsils/wisdom teeth out. S/he is lying in bed, feeling bored and looking like a chipmunk. Sure, you could simply hand out flowers and a card and be on your merry way. Or you could relocate poker night to your friend's bedside: if Muhammad can't come to the party, the party must come to Muhammad. Now that's the way to be a caring, considerate friend!

friends visiting from out of town

Because you are known far and wide as the sexiest bitch around, your friends will flock from all corners of the globe to hang with you. This means that you must have a tour ready for them. Think of all of the silly things that you can show them in your area, and hit the road for a day filled with arcane local trivia and festivities. Make sure your itinerary includes opportunities for adult refreshment along the way: brewery tours, wine tastings, etc. Throw in some fabulous shopping sites, too.

weddings

Okay, so you may be surprised to see weddings classified as "mundane," but hey, if it's not your wedding, who really cares about it? Still, weddings have a reputation as excellent places to hook up, and I totally believe this. I have a number of friends who met their beloveds at weddings, so don't write these shindigs off completely as a conspiracy against single people. In order to make things slide your way, there are a few critical things that you must pack in your bag before every wedding: a rockin' dance mix tape, temporary tattoos, a shaker of salt, and condoms. (The last one is obvious, but I thought I'd remind you.)

So when you're surrounded by wreaths of baby's breath and all of the relatives are getting their groove on to a CD that sounds remarkably like the soundtrack to "Sweatin' to the Oldies," it's time to rescue the event from being D.O.A. What are you supposed to do? First of all, swap out the dreadful compilation that Uncle Stan made in 1952 and throw in one of your mixes that is bound to shake things up a little.

Second, carry fake tattoos. That's right, it's time to save those poor bridesmaids from their peach chiffon dresses and make them look a little more hell on wheels. Sure, venomous snakes and flaming guitars may not be what the bride had in mind for the demure arms of her bridesmaids. Hopefully she's so preoccupied with staring deeply into the eyes of her newly betrothed and she won't notice that her bridesmaids suddenly look like a group of Hell's Belles.

It's also time to make those groomsmen earn their keep. They should be dancing like maniacs, so do whatever it takes to get those guys loosened up. Ties wrapped around the forehead send a clear message that the wearer is wild, while simultaneously doubling as sweatbands. Nice.

The bar is a critical weapon in your arsenal. Shots are mandatory at weddings; preferably you should cajole as many people into drinking them as possible. You can keep it simple and go with the classic: tequila body shots. Lick a part of someone else's body, use your salt shaker and douse the area with salt, lick the salt off your partner, do a shot of tequila, and then finish by biting into a slice of lime.

another sexy bitch has a baby

I'm sure many women find it appalling that this event is classified as "mundane" but oh well. Having a baby is a critical moment in a woman's life, and not for all the obvious reasons, like she brings life into the world, yadda, yadda, yadda. It goes deeper than all of that mumbo jumbo; having a baby can be the death knell of the existence of a sexy bitch.

Consider it your mission to keep her in the land of the party womanimals. I admit that this is daunting mission because your friend is victim to all kinds of crazy hormones, fears of inadequacy, and sleep deprivation, but you must overcome all of this. She will thank you later (and her partner will thank you even sooner). It's not a great idea to show up at the hospital ready to commence this transformation. Hospital staff members have these silly notions that dance music, magnums, and raucous laughter are not appreciated in the maternity ward, so avoid this confrontation and give your friend a few days to recuperate.

After sufficient time has passed, bring the party to her. You and a few compadres must bring over dinner and drinks so that she does not forget that drinks don't have to have nipples attached. (Unless your friend has announced that she's not planning to breastfeed at all, and both she and her baby are ready to hit the bottle, make sure you bring fun non-alcoholic drinks for the nursing mom.) Bring some good music and provide her with a few hours of gossip (with a liberal sprinkling of scandal) and tasty treats. Since she has only been wearing clothing that resembles camping tents, bring over some fashion magazines and get her back up to speed on what is considered trendy and hip. Remind her gently that anything that involves ruffled bloomers should be avoided in adult sizes. Up the dosage and frequency of these events over the next few months until she is back to her former haute mama self.

7 the world's your oyster: unconventional places to party

True party mavens know that you don't have to be in a bar or a club after dark to party: a sexy bitch can party anywhere. So where are you supposed to be doing this? Yeah, if you're standing in your local bar, The Man Hole, for the third weekend in a row, it's time to seriously rethink your choice in venues (and possibly a few other things, but that's for another book).

the office

It's mind-numbing that we have to spend most of our waking hours cooped up in an office. But instead of dwelling on this injustice and loathing everything about your job, concentrate on the fact that your job enables you to party. In essence, your workplace is a blank easel and you are Picasso. That's right, it is up to YOU to make your office a happening place to work and play. If you play things just right, you will move beyond merely going out after work on Thursday nights and spilling $10 martinis on all of the other working stiffs to bring a much-needed festive flair to your job. Oh, and if that's not enough, you'll probably get your fine self promoted. Who's the boss going to pick to move up the ranks: the boring wallflower who quietly collects kitten postcards on her cubicle wall or the sexy bitch who has her finger on the pulse of the hottest happenings? Gee, this is a tough one. (Note: if the kitten postcard types are the ones getting promoted, you need to throw two weeks notice out the window and get out of there as fast as you can.)

Before we get too carried away with locating a spot on the office ceiling for a disco ball, consider your company's culture and make sure that you're not going to ruffle the feathers of the head honchos by introducing a party attitude to the cubicle jungle. Ask yourself the following questions: what do your coworkers seem to do as 5:00 approaches on a Thursday or Friday evening? Is there a quiet buzz about the latest releases at Blockbuster, or does there seem to be a sense of longing lingering in the air? Perhaps these clueless people do not know how to channel excitement. This is where you come in.

STEP 1: Make your desk a party waiting to go off. Have a calendar on your wall with everyone's birthday and make a big deal whenever one comes along. Bring in some special snacks, and you'll be the center of attention (remember: the birthday guy or gal is really just a front for YOU to grab a moment in the spotlight!). And don't merely rely on the obvious reasons to celebrate. Did someone just get a fabulous new haircut? Go ahead and grab a posse to go out for lunch. Be sure to recognize more subtle occasions to party, such as recognizing someone who just ran a marathon, bought a new house, ditched a lame boyfriend, or whatever. Make sure that your desk is the place to be for gossip and socializing. If you're afraid it will look like you never do any work, consider this: you're the funniest and wildest sexy bitch around, and everyone will want to be in your good graces. Your boss will be impressed because all of your coworkers will soon want your opinion and help on just about everything.

STEP 2: Check with your boss and see if you can become the editor-in-chief of the soon-to-be-created office newsletter. These can be extremely annoying if left in the hands of someone less qualified, but your wit, spunk, and critical eye will make your publication the toast of the office. What should be covered in the newsletter? Recount any office news, such as birthdays, new babies, and weddings, but make sure you throw a sassy spin on everything so it doesn't read like a Hallmark card. Add pictures and be sure to write captions underneath that will mildly mock everyone. The key is not to do all of the work yourself: instead, email everyone that you are looking for contributors and people will clamor to get involved. In fact, you may be amazed by the creativity of some of your coworkers.

STEP 3: Coordinate social events. This does not have to be much work, so don't fret. Simply set some after-hours get-togethers at local bars and restaurants. Better yet, call any local museums and see if a tour can be put together for everyone after work or send an email out asking if everyone wants to get tickets to a local sporting event. You should be the catalyst for getting people to think about interesting and fun things to do after work. Before you know it, your officemates will surprise you: someone will offer to take people out on their boat when no one even knew he had one.

STEP 4: Set up some office competitions. Are the Oscars coming up? Put together an Oscar pool and get everyone to chip in $5 so there can be lotto for the winner. Get people interested in starting up some office team that really is a disguise for drinking on an athletic field somewhere. Is there a bar nearby with a dart board or something? Set up a competition for an evening after work. Once again, people will rise to the occasion and start coming up with ideas too: you won't have to be the lone workhorse for long.

So this all sounds super, but what do you do if your office is lame and you doubt your bosses will encourage any of this type of activity? First of all, assume nothing and ask your boss. You should point out that productivity rises when people feel comfortable and are enjoying the company of their coworkers. In this age of job hopping, employers should be open to thinking up creative ways to engage their workers. If you get shot down by the boss, tell them you'll miss them and pack your stuff up. You've got better places to go.

the gym

Okay, so sometimes you feel light on sexy and heavy on bitch when you're oozing sweat by the buckets and wheezing in your workout tights, but the gym can be a great place to party. Have you ever noticed that gyms are packed with cute men working on their abs? If your gym does not have any hot prospects, I highly recommend shopping around for a gym with a little more possibility. Once you are going to the gym with some interesting men, you'll find it's easy to strike up conversation. Ask for help returning some weights to the stand, ask for someone to spot for you, or simply ask for directions from some appealing guy.

Demand that your gym include classes that are actually fun and help you to lose some poundage. Dancing, kickboxing, biking, cross-training, and rock climbing classes can all be surprisingly good times with a good instructor and some kickass tunes.

Finally, add some originality to your workout clothes. Sparkles can be bought at any craft store and should be poured liberally onto all tank tops and shorts. Sew, staple, or glue (depending on your craftiness level) some sequins, feathers, or fake fur to T-shirts to bring a bit of glamour to an otherwise unglamorous outfit.

museums, parks, zoos, and aquariums

Check the culture and arts section of the local newspaper to see what interesting events are happening near you. You'll be amazed at all of the places to party that aren't bars and restaurants. Many museums are open late one evening during the week, and they often have live music and bars for you to enjoy with your fine arts. Many concert halls have special concerts that you can attend for free too. During the warmer months, zoos and parks tend to sponsor concerts and you can pack a picnic basket and let the good times roll! Many different non-profit organizations sponsor fundraising parties at interesting venues, such as aquariums and planetariums, that can provide a fun change of scenery. You may even learn something, and you'll definitely have the opportunity to meet some new people.

sporting events

Attending a professional athletic event, such as an NBA or NFL game, can easily cost you over a hundred bucks after you've paid for parking, admission, and concessions—ugh! Granted, it's fun to see men trotting around in tight uniforms, but there are cheaper ways of doing this…and some of them will let you get much closer to the action!

First of all, you can always join a co-ed sports league, like a softball, soccer, or bowling league. This is a great way to meet men and party, because usually there is an emphasis on indulging in frosty adult beverages before, during, or after practices and games. Plus, you will get in shape!

Another option is training for a race or event with a group. Tons of different charity organizations train people for marathons, triathlons, and bike races, and these are great places to meet new people, get in shape, and even support a good cause (other than yourself!). You can become the social organizer of your group and arrange all of the after-practice parties at local watering holes. Or you can even bring refreshments in your party mobile to the actual practice site and host a party al fresco at the track or park. And once you've actually completed whatever event you are training for, you can have a big party to celebrate the accomplishment. Many races finish with beer gardens and other fun party options, so don't let a little sweat dissuade you from an opportunity for a good time!

Many cities also have minor league teams, and these can be great games to attend because they're cheaper and more casual. Remember *Bull Durham* and how much fun they had in the minor leagues? You can turn a minor event into a major party with a festive attitude and a backpack filled with snacks and drinks. You'll also find it's easy to mingle with the players at these smaller venues. Who knows, you may be able to score a home run with that cute catcher who's actually close enough to see your sultry winks!

your Car

Yes, yes, your car is a mode of transportation, but it can double as a party mobile. That's right, throw some lounge chairs and a cooler in the back and be ready to take this fiesta to the freeways. Some narrow-minded people assume that tailgating can only happen at sporting events, yet this interpretation of tailgating is way too confining. There is absolutely no reason why you cannot have a mini happy hour out of the trunk of your car anywhere.

The guys who redesigned the Volkswagen Bug figured out the party life and had their car sport a flower vase; get your rig one! Just tape it to the dashboard or something, but let's decorate. Keep photos in your sun visor and candy in the glove compartment to keep up the spirits of fellow motorists stuck in traffic. Incidentally, handing out candy to someone you've just met in a minor fender bender is a sure-fire way to improve the situation.

When you and your compadres have located a spot that calls for some partying, simply pull out the beach chairs, hoist open the cooler, and unload the snacks and beverages. Be sure to tuck a festive table-cloth in the cooler so you can really bring the scene together by throwing the tablecloth over the cooler and using it as a table. Don't forget to have some good tunes in the tape deck or CD player. Once your car has the right ingredients, you can zip off to parks or scenic overlooks and kick back. In fact, you don't even need to leave the driveway to have a good time. I had some neighbors who used to keep their boat parked in the driveway, and it was always the center of festivities. In fact, I'm not sure if the boat ever even made it to water, because we were all just chilling on it in the driveway and having a great time.

Okay—I shouldn't have to tell you, but if your car's the party mobile and you'll have to drive it somewhere soon, don't drink. Or drink some fun fruity drink with a tropical parasol that is sans alcohol. Or make some other person drive and don't let them drink. Do not ruin your evening by ending it in the emergency room—that's one place that is tough to turn into a party.

8 a night out on the town

While it's fun to host your own party, it's also fun to get out and see and be seen. A night out can be as easy as meeting friends at a local watering hole for some snacks—or it can involve a bacchanalian multi-stop evening of indulgence with drinks, dinner, and dancing. Aside from waiting in long bathroom lines, usually the biggest bummer about heading out for a night is that it's going to involve spending vast sums of money. But this doesn't have to be the case, especially if you know how to work it to score free drinks and other bonuses.

restaurants

Everyone loves some tasty chow, daring conversation, and strong drinks, so head to your favorite restaurant. If you love novelty (not that kind of novelty—you and your dirty mind!), you may want to start a restaurant club with your friends: make a pact to try a new restaurant together every week or month. A few factors are key to having a successful sexy bitch night out at a restaurant. First, avoid all family restaurants and any place where the servers wear buttons that say inane things like "Ask me about the best burger in town!" These horribly embarrassing accessories tend to be worn by perky acne-scarred teens accustomed to serving harried moms and dads toting brats who won't stop demanding free refills all night. These are exactly the types of establishments you want to avoid.

Instead, hone in on a destination with gorgeous servers, interesting and unique dishes that you don't typically make at home, low lighting, appealing background music, and interesting decor. Or a funky neighborhood place that serves exotic food or has comfy booths. Just be sure to choose a place where you can hang out and your server won't try to speed you out the door; the party can't simmer to perfection when your meal's done in half an hour and other diners are eyeing your table like vultures.

A promising technique to ensure your table receives excellent service is to make it clear that your party is going to want a steady supply of drinks all night long. Second, ask your server what dishes they recommend. Sometimes they will try to upsell you by pushing the priciest thing on the menu, but you will probably find that most servers give you a genuine response about their favorites. Plus, it shows that you respect their expertise and everyone enjoys feeling smart. Third, invite them to have a shot with you or some dessert or something. Now obviously this one won't work at a swanky joint where the serving staff is too uptight to join your group in a bit of silliness, but it can bring on a scene of high hilarity if your server gets in on the act and treats you to specials from the kitchen and bar.

clubs

The biggest deterrent to clubbing is the lame part about waiting outside in the sleet while you wait for the bouncers who look like extras straight out of "The Sopranos" to bestow a nod in your direction to indicate that you and your posse are in. Of course, then there is usually a steep cover fee. If you're not arriving at one of these places with P. Diddy on one side and Beyoncé on the other, you need a strategy to get in quickly and with minimal hemorrhaging of cash. The best method is to cultivate a set of friends—deejays, musicians, bartenders, etc.—who can comp you at the clubs they frequent. It's a fair trade: your fabulous friendship for freebies. You can also try listening for radio station giveaways, although the odds of winning may be even smaller than the speck of kindness in a bouncer's heart. When all else fails, people have been known to make stuff up. I'm not naming names, but I've heard of people getting around haughty bouncers by giving themselves fake careers. Some say they're the entertainment columnist for a local paper, or a writer on assignment for magazine X. Others claim to be a location scout for a movie studio, or even a producer for a reality television show prowling for "talent." Supposedly these big fat liars have received tons of special treatment as club staff tries to razzle dazzle them—it's pathetic how desperate some people are for their fifteen minutes of fame.

As far as scoring some free drinks in one of these joints, your best bet is to use your sexy bitch attitude to make it clear that you are not a woman who is typically stuck having to bother with something as menial as ordering drinks. Sidle up to the bar but don't get right up to it where you will actually have to order. Stand with your posse and send the vibe by laughing and casually scanning the area. Be selective about making eye contact, because a look that rests a second too long on the wrong fellow could set you up for an evening of fending off a guy who has the wrong idea. Invariably if you look like you are having a good time, someone will come up and offer some beverages. If the guy looks like he has possibility, keep him within range and get some dancing in. If the guy seems a little annoying, enjoy the free drink and then take advantage of the crowds and loud music to become distracted and eventually lose him.

bars

Bars come in all shapes and sizes, and I highly recommend sampling as many as possible so that you can figure out what you like. Personally, I have a wide range of bar tastes; I like everything from swilling down a few dark beers at a pub, to eyeing row after colorful row of gleaming liquor bottles at a swankier spot, to downing a few brews at a local divey sports bar. It's always nice when you and your posse can own the bar. No, I don't mean really investing in one, and cleaning up countless beer spills; instead I mean reigning queen supreme in one. Having this type of power is usually best accomplished by staging a mini-invasion. You and your sexy bitch retinue need to descend en masse and make it so that everything that happens in that spot must meet your approval. How do you accomplish such a daring task? Easy: wear your hottest ensemble, round up the gals, hit a spot that you want to claim as your own, and demand top-notch service. This is easiest to accomplish at a place that is staffed mostly by men. These guys are usually thrilled to have a break from the same old beefcakes lining their barstools and giving stingy tips. You and your friends will dazzle the staff with your charm and have them right where you want them. Establish a routine evening where you and the posse get together for some cocktails and a show or something. Just do me a favor and avoid the hackneyed Monday Night Football Outing. Instead opt for a girls' night that involves a cheesy television show or a night of games. You all can get your groove on by playing cards, pool, dice, or darts.

Aside from the obvious joys of people-watching, having a multitude of alcoholic beverages at your disposal, and not having to clean up afterward, bars are a terrific spot for playing games—not just playing hard to get with your flavor of the month, but actually getting competitive with some bar games!

Is there anything sexier than beating people at their own game? I don't think so. Oh, and when I say "people" I am talking about the lesser sex—the group of Neanderthals we call our boyfriends or husbands, or maybe that lecherous bald guy eyeing you from the end of the bar. There are really three things that men have held over our heads since the dawn of time: peeing while standing up, beer bellies, and bar games. Well, the lasses of *The Full Monty* showed us that we are up to the task of peeing while standing, dudes can keep their beer bellies, and I am here to pull back the curtain on men and their rabid addiction to games.

The games you might come across at any bar fall into three categories: 1) pool, 2) darts, 3) video. In the interest of time I am going to skip over video games, because more often than not any guy playing video games at a bar is most likely underage—he's just trying to keep out of the sight-line of the bartender until he becomes so intoxicated he bellows out his hatred of Blinky the Ghost (of Ms. PacMan fame) and at that time is escorted out of the bar by the nape of his neck. But some of your best times can be wasted partaking in the other bar games.

The information below is just to get you in the game. If you find you are actually rather good at these games and are interested in learning the strategies, maybe you can get a private lesson from that cute guy who's getting ready to rack his balls for another game of pool. I told you these games can be fun! It's time to get a little more savvy when it comes to ball games...

billiards (or pool)

The most common type of pool is 8-ball. The object is to hit in all of your balls and the black 8- ball before your opponent. As you'll be able to tell when you approach the table, the balls are separated into two types, stripes and solids. This game is easy and you are sure to own the table once you have refined your stroke. The first place you can announce yourself with authority is when you sign up to play. If there isn't a sign-up sheet or chalkboard, then you will probably notice that there are quarters lined up against the inside of one of the rails. These little piles are not for taking, but instead act as placehold-ers for the folks who are waiting to play. If you don't figure out how people are keeping track of who is up next, it won't matter how many times you have watched *The Color of Money* to hone your pool-shark skills—because you won't ever get on the table.

the rack

If someone yells "rack 'em," don't suddenly grab for your breast thinking, "Yes, on second thought this blouse does show too much cleavage." They are referring to the beginning of the game when you put all of the balls in the wooden or plastic triangle also known as the rack. And here's a word of advice: the rack is often "hidden" at one end of the pool table either in a slot or hanging on a hook under the table. Knowing this might save you the embarrassment of hunting around the bar looking for the rack like you are in the middle of a one-girl Easter Egg Hunt.

At first glance you might think that the balls have been randomly placed into the rack, and if women had been the first to play billiards, the balls would be randomly placed in the rack to speed up the pace of the game. But men love to dilly-dally over their games for days at a time (please check out a sport like cricket and/or baseball if you doubt this statement). And even more than dithering over games, men spend a lot of time fondling balls, both athletic balls and those things jingling and jangling between their legs. But I digress... Anyway, the most important thing is to put the 8-ball in the "middle" of the rack. The "middle" is considered the middle spot in the third row from the top. The second most significant piece of rack etiquette is to rotate between solid and striped balls. So you start with a solid ball at the top, then two striped balls, and then solid balls on either side of the 8-ball, and on the fourth and fifth rows you alternate solid and striped balls. If you want to get ultra-professional (bordering on ultra-anal) you can put the one ball at the top and the two and three ball at the other two corners. But if you remember to put the 8-ball in the middle you are looking pretty good.

Your next question is probably, "Where do I put this triangle of balls?" (Not a question you likely ask every day, unless you have an even wilder social life than mine!) If you look closely at the table, there should be two little round markers on the felt near each end of the table. You put the top of the triangle on one marker and remove the triangle.

the pool cue and cue ball

Those long sticks hanging on the wall by the pool table are pool cues. You hold the fat end firmly in your hot little fist and slide the other end lightly through the space on the back of your other hand between the thumb and index finger, whacking it into balls to send them across the table. This can be tricky, but lessons on form are a great excuse to get some hot guy to put his arms around you and show you how it's done.

The catch to pool is that you don't just hit your balls straight into the pocket—no, that would be too simple. Instead, you have to hit the cue ball (the little white ball) so that IT hits another ball. Playing pool, you might find for the first time in your life you mutter the phrase "I wish I had paid more attention in my high school geometry class!!" because at the base of billiards you are trying to move round objects around a table by hitting them at the correct angles. From here on out, you will try to hit the cue ball at such an angle that it will career into the intended stripe or solid ball and this ball will hopefully end up in one of the six pockets on the table.

When you have a long rod at your disposal and you've been steadily consuming frosty adult beverages for the better part of an evening, it's very tempting to treat your pool cue as a plaything, such as a ninja weapon, a microphone, or a sex toy. Whether or not you actually give in to this temptation is a tough call. I have seen this go horribly wrong when my drinking buddy Lavern had the crowd going as she showcased her high school drill team moves, whirling like a dervish until the grand finale was cut short when the butt of her cue knocked out the front tooth of our waitress. On the flipside, after five kamikazes it is nearly impossible not to treat the cue as a phallic appendage, so go ahead and do it... preferably when your boyfriend isn't looking. On the other hand he might enjoy it, so go for it.

the break

You're finally ready to start playing! Usually the winner from the last game has the honor of "breaking." So let's assume that's you. Take the cue ball and go to the opposite end of the table from the racked-up triangle of balls. You'll notice there's another marker similar to the one you just used to line up the rack. Put the cue ball on the marker or anywhere behind the imaginary line that intersects it, and smack the cue ball into the triangle to break it apart and scatter the balls around the table. (Hence the name "break.") One way to check whether your ball is behind the imaginary line is to lay your pool stick across the width of the table while intersecting the marker on the pool table. This is also known as "the kitchen check" (don't ask me), and becomes more frequent as the night goes on and your eyesight begins to get a little fuzzy.

do you have solid balls, or stripey balls?

Okay: somebody broke, and the balls are scattered across the table. If the table is "open" that means nobody has hit in a ball and you are free to zero in on either a strip or solid and hit it into one of the pockets. Let's say you hit in a solid ball: from here on out you are trying to knock in solid balls. It goes both ways: if your opponent knocks in a solid or stripe, by default you are trying to knock in the other class of balls. Once you have hit in all of your balls, the final hurdle is to hit in the 8-ball.

scratch

You "scratch" when the cue ball accidentally ends up in one of the pockets. This happens surprisingly often considering how difficult it can be to actually hit any of your own balls into those seemingly large pockets! If you do scratch, you lose your turn. If you are playing at a bar, once a ball is down (you've hit it into a pocket) it is locked in the internal workings of the table and won't be freed again until the next player inserts her quarters to release the balls for a new game. However, if you're playing at somebody's house it might be house rules to penalize players for scratching by making them pull a ball they already hit in a pocket and put it back on the table. (It goes on one of those little markers we talked about before.) But this can lead to epic length games, so I recommend adhering to "bar rules" of not pulling balls out for scratches.

slop

This really is the one area where you can separate yourself from the general public. Slop is when you accidentally knock in one of your balls. The best way to test if you just made a slop shot is if you hear yourself saying "I meant to do that" to an audience of eye-rollers. In general, if you made a slop shot, the ball you just hit in can stay down but you lose your turn.

darts

For my money, darts is a much-underappreciated way to waste a few hours or days at your favorite local pub. What other activity encourages you to keep a cocktail in one hand, hold a conversation with the bartender, and throw sharp objects around the bar all at the same time?

One of the more helpful things I can share about darts is that for some reason it is much easier to remove the darts from the board if you spin the darts clockwise while removing them. I have no idea why this is, but it is true particularly for the ever-more-popular plastic boards. It takes a feat of superhuman strength to remove the darts by pulling them straight out, but if you give them a little clockwise twist they come spinning right out.

I wish I could give you a pointer that made hitting the bullseye as easy, but I can't. Still, remember my earlier point that you can hold your drink while playing, so that makes practicing much more enjoyable. My one piece of strategic advice for novices is always to aim for the bullseye (the center), and then if you miss it (which you will almost always) there is a better chance that your off-target darts might hit one of the areas you are supposed to be aiming at. This may not sound like the best advice, but when you are just starting out it's hard enough to consistently hit the board and not the other patrons of the bar, without adding the stress of wondering every time "Now, what am I aiming at again?" Just get up there, launch your three darts, and let somebody else keep score.

Since you will get better, it might be helpful to learn the rules. Here's an easy dart game to start with: 501. The most complicated thing about the dart game 501 is there is a little math involved. Each player begins with a score of 501 and tries to be the first to get to exactly 0. If your dart hits the inner bullseye (good luck!) it's worth 50 points, and the outer bullseye is worth 25. Those little numbers around the outside of the dart board tell you how many points hitting each pie wedge on the board is worth. Now you are probably wondering about the two rings. I'm glad you asked. The outer ring is the "double" ring: if you throw a dart into that area, your score is doubled. Therefore, if you throw a dart in the outer ring area of the 20 pie wedge, you have just hit 2x20, for 40 points. The inner ring is the "triple" ring, and if you throw a dart into the inner ring of the 20 pie wedge, you have just thrown a triple 20, for 60 points. That's another beautiful thing about darts: once you understand the scoring, it actually makes sense. Imagine that, a game that men came up with that actually makes sense!!

So let's say the game begins, you launch your darts at the board, and you score a 5, a double 6, and a 14. Your score for that round would be [5+(2x6)+14]=31, so you would subtract 31 from 501 for a total score of 470. You would begin your next turn at 470, and keep trying to whittle down your score until you get to 0. The one big wrinkle is that if you don't hit 0 exactly, you have to go back to whatever score you had at the beginning of that turn. So let's say you had played for a while and your score stood at 35 at the beginning of your turn. You would be doing okay if you hit a 20 and then a 10, but if you hit anything higher than a 5 next, your score would go back to 35 (so close but so far!!). Here's the good news: with electronic dart boards becoming so popular, you can leave the addition and subtraction to the machine and focus on taking in the sights and sounds of your local pub.

I do truly enjoy a good game of darts. An added bonus is that there are very few aphrodisiacs as strong as a sexy bitch strolling into a bar and holding court at the pool table or dart board.

9   tips for the hostess

Now you know how to party anywhere—how about your place? Here are some tips on being the hostess with the mostest fun and the leastest work.

outfitting party central

Whether you live in a studio apartment or a mansion, sexy bitches can make any space a party place. Avoid clutter and embrace minimalism so that you can squeeze more partyers into your crib. Many people love to decorate by buying everything in cream and beige (call it the anti-decorating decor), but this makes your space a blank canvas for someone to start coloring with red wine stains and guacamole streaks. So unless you live for cleaning and bleaching all the time, dare to be wild and actually decorate your pad with color. Choose rich colors that stains can blend into easily. Another option is to slipcover your upholstered furniture, but this can get pricey. The key is to keep all of your furniture simple and easy to maintain. When you're hosting, you don't want to be worrying the whole time that someone is going to drip chocolate sauce all over your beige carpet— talk about a buzz kill for you and your guests.

Throw out the old beer can mobiles and beer bongs that are treasured souvenirs from your college days. Your "National Lampoon" era is over, and we are trying to migrate into a more mature direction. Even if you don't act like a grownup all the time, it's time to take a deep breath and realize that you are one. It's still okay to shop at Ikea, but you may want to stash the catalog away out of view of your public.

Your easiest party option is always to have some people over for dinner. You don't even need to cook—think takeout! But if you don't have enough space or cash to afford a long dining room table, simply go out and buy a few café-size folding tables and chairs. Big groups around tables are overrated anyway, because it's easy to get sick of the person sitting next to you all night. Seating your guests at smaller tables encourages group conversations, and people can always hop from table to table to socialize. Go for the easy el cheapo tables: they can be covered up with cute tablecloths, according to your party theme, and you can easily fold them up and stash them away in between hosting.

If you do have some cash, invest in one piece of quality furniture. Otherwise buy a couple of colorful accessories to bring some originality to your pad. Photographs are always great decoration, and they're cheap and show your friends how important they are to you. Be creative: use funky frames and colorful matting to make the photos look more interesting than they would stuck in a clear plastic frame. Toss out the old lava lamp from your dorm room and make your place look like an adult with good taste lives there.

Because your parties will be the best ever, make sure you have plenty of bedding in your linen closets (or jammed under your bed, whatever). You don't want to encourage your buds to hit the road after drinking, so have them spend the night instead. If your overnight guests know how to whip up a mean omelet in the morning, they will have earned their keep! Plus, when you wake up with other people, you can wrangle some help cleaning up out of them and not be stuck doing all of the grunt work yourself.

party commandments

Consider a few basic rules to ensure that you enjoy yourself and stay sane while hosting…

1. chow something down before the party

It's easy to get stuck chit chatting with your guests as they begin to arrive and the next thing you know, all of the potstickers have been scarfed down by your lovable (albeit freeloading) friends. Plus, your endurance for drinking margaritas will be greatly enhanced with some food in you, and the likelihood of "snacks for later" (a.k.a. food in your teeth) is minimized.

2. sample any mixed drink recipes before guests arrive

After you have eaten something, start tasting your margaritas, punch, or whatever concoction you are brewing. Some people disagree with this rule because it means you run the risk of being the most inebriated person at your own soiree, but personally I've never thought this is a big problem since you're the queen of your own castle and any minion who criticizes is off the invite list.

3. enlist your friends as paparazzi

Documenting the evening's progress with photos is always a good idea, both to help you relive the night's highlights the next day and to blackmail any friends who engaged in illicit activities. If you're lucky, someone will sneak some anonymous nude pictures that you will get to enjoy when you check out the film later. (As a general rule of thumb, whenever you see an idle camera lying around at weddings and high school reunions, you should always sneak away briefly and snap some illicit headless close-up nude shots for the owner to be surprised by later. Consider it a belated party favor that someone will really appreciate.) Video cameras can also be fun at parties. In fact, a successful filmmaker friend of mine attributes her current cinematic success to the "drunkumentaries" she made in her earlier years.

4. key party props include a cowboy hat and feather boa

Use the cowboy hat to collect people's car keys when they show up, so you can cut off any drunken lout who dares to propose driving home from your party. The hat can also serve as an excellent bowl for games that require players to choose a slip of paper, etc. The necessity of a boa should be obvious. First of all, everyone looks fabulous in a boa and it tends to make the wearer feel extraordinarily glamorous. Or tie it to a door knob and something else to open a door that tends to close and shut out revelers. And if you're still not convinced of the importance of the boa, try using it as a fetching leash for an over-friendly cat or dog.

5. party proof your house or apartment

This includes rolling up rugs, putting away any odds and ends that you don't want manhandled by the public, and setting out ample toilet paper in the bathroom so you don't get any unpleasant surprises when you're towel drying your hair the next day.

6. have good tunes on hand to keep the party humming

Of course, music is the obvious way to turn a ho-hum time into a kickass party, and with all of the options to download music, there is really no excuse not to have great tunes. You can also invite friends to bring some of their own CDs to ensure that you have an eclectic selection. For your planning pleasure, here's a music list guaranteed to keep people dancing...

> **MUSIC PARADE**
>
> ### greatest hits from sexy bitches
>
> "Push It" by Salt n Pepa
>
> "Take It Off" by The Donnas
>
> "If I Were a Rich Girl" by Gwen Stefani
>
> "Bad Reputation" by Joan Jett
>
> "Fighter" by Christina Aguilera
>
> "Respect" by Aretha Franklin
>
> "Independent" by Destiny's Child
>
> "I Will Survive" by Gloria Gaynor
>
> "Into the Groove" by Madonna
>
> "Complicated" by Avril Lavigne
>
> "Bitch" by Meredith Brooks
>
> "Ladies First" by Queen Latifah
>
> "Last Dance" by Donna Summer

7. your kitchen must have a few essential tools

It's fine if you're using forks that are missing tongs and eating off chipped plates, but there are a few things that no sexy bitch's kitchen is without.

- It goes without saying that you must have a bottle opener (the type that opens both beer and wine, please).
- A blender is essential for whipping up margaritas and easy dips like hummus. In addition to the obvious tasks for which these handy dandy little appliances were designed, blenders can be excellent noisemakers when your upstairs or downstairs neighbors are obnoxious and need to be wakened at unusual times or if you are on the phone with someone who you want to ditch; simply turn the blender on full tilt and stop everyone in their tracks.
- No kitchen is complete without a microwave to heat things up and make popcorn in no time.
- You should also have some shot glasses and different types of glasses, like martini glasses, highballs, champagne flutes. Beer mugs are optional, since nobody minds swigging straight out of the bottle.
- And the most important sexy bitch kitchen tool? Lots of take-out menus.

8. no dish divas allowed

Okay, so you may not be able to get away without doing any dishes, but give yourself a break and go with plastic or paper plates. (The rainforest will survive just this once.) Your flirting and chatting time will be seriously curtailed if you hide your fabulous manicure in dish gloves. Many stores carry cute plates that can lend a festive air to any occasion, and you will be extremely happy when you wake up the next day and don't find towers of dishes looming over you.

9. give the hood some say and keep the cops away

Make sure you invite your neighbors to your shindig. That's right, even if you live next door to the Munsters. Trust me, it's much better to conduct a preemptive strike and have the neighbors over than it is to find yourself face to face with local law enforcement. If the cops do show up, invite them to join the party! (It's worth a try.)

10. post cab numbers by the door

No one wants to send a friend off into a dangerous situation, so encourage your friends to spend the night at your place (especially if they are male!) or insist that they take a cab home if you think they have overindulged.

11. don't be obsessed with cleanliness

Unless you have invited Mr. Clean to your soiree, there is no reason to stay overly concerned about keeping your place clean while you have people over. Consider hosting a party a good excuse to do a thorough cleaning—but save it for the next afternoon. Roll up any rugs you may be concerned about and stop worrying about spills, shoes, etc. Let people have a good time and keep your blood pressure at a healthy level. No one wants the host chasing them around with a dustpan all night.

12. beverages should be served in bottles, cans, or plastic cups

Kegs are not very convenient when it comes to hosting a party. The pumps can easily get jammed, and next thing you know, you have a dry party. In addition, kegs tend to make a gigantic foamy mess all over the floor. You may feel like you're not being environmentally conscious with bottles all over the place, but you can always take them to a recycle center. Better yet, get a friend to do it.

13. have a party pet

You need a party animal in your life…literally. When you choose a pet, try to find one with an outgoing personality—not a cat who hides under the bed at the drop of a hat or a dog who growls at new friends! Keep your dog or cat used to meeting new people: you want an animal who's as much of an extrovert as you are. Some people say when you get a new dog it's supposed to meet at least 100 people in the first few weeks. What better excuse for a party?

Dogs and cats should always be wearing collars that show that they too enjoy a good time. Toss out the lame nylon collar and indulge your furry friend with a colorfully decorated collar and leash. So you're wondering how you can make your goldfish look like the partyer that it really is? Put some fun trinkets, like a mini disco ball or funky beads or marbles, into its tank.

14. make your guest roster A-list

Putting together the right party to make your party a success is a fine art. I don't want to scare you, but you can put together a fabulous party and have it sunk by a bunch of duds. So, what's a hostess to do? Well, get out your address book and let's see who makes the cut.

Go heavy on the men. This statement can be interpreted in all kinds of ways, and I don't want to limit you, but my point here is to INVITE a lot of men. Hot men. So how do you locate all of these gems? Network, network, network. Ask your guy friends to bring more guys. Hell, join a co-ed sports team (soccer, touch football, skiing, etc.) or an all-women team that is connected to a men's league and invite all of these weekend warriors to your shindig. Even better, get your hot little paws on an email list for one of these sports teams and send out an invite (daring, but possibly ingenious!).

Invite your favorite sexy bitches and work out a hunting code in advance. Have signals so that you know which gal has her eye on which prize and work as a team. Have a little pre-funk with your pals so you can all loosen up, gossip, and try the food and drinks in advance. If someone has some great clothing encourage her to bring a few goodies to help out with wardrobe.

If you are single and looking to mingle, be selective when it comes to inviting couples. If you have limited space and you and your single friends are looking for some action, don't clutter up the place with people who are unavailable. Preferably you want to invite attached friends who can bring along some interesting single possibilities. In fact, you may want to make this their condition for entry!

Try to invite a friend with great taste in tunes who isn't afraid to be your deejay. This way you can actually work the floor more and leave the spinning to a pro.

Okay, so this isn't exactly the kindest thing to add, but no party is complete without a lush or two. These partyers serve as your "rabbit"—they run ahead and stir up the action. For one thing, they get the party swinging and get everyone to loosen up because it's clear that they will be the ones who take it for the team and end up doing the embarrassing things that save everyone else from worrying that they will be "that guy" or "that girl." Voila, pressure's off everyone else. Just don't tell them what their role is since you don't want to psych them out and have them underperform.

15. get the word out

Even with email quickly replacing all forms of handwritten communication, it's still a good idea to send out invitations, either electronically or by using old-fashioned snail mail. With all of those wads of bills and credit card notices that smother my mailbox daily, I look forward to receiving mail from a real person I actually know! I confess to being partial to the novelty of receiving a cute invitation in the mail that I can post on my wall, but sometimes a party is put together so hastily that things must be done over email. Initially I thought all of those companies that put together email invites were very clever, but now they annoy me with their self-promotional surveys and membership requests. Whatever!

So, what info needs to get on an invitation?

• **Name of host or hosts.** (duh)

• **Date.** Depending on the size and intricacy of your party, be sure to send out invitations well in advance. Usually three to four weeks ahead of date is safe, but check the calendar to make sure there aren't any other big events the same day or night as your bender.

• **Time.** When you're figuring out the time for your event, think carefully. If you're serving a sit-down dinner, you don't want a bunch of clowns showing up overly fashionably late and arriving in the middle of dessert, do you? If you are working with a fairly tight timeline, be clear about it in your invitation. You can say something like: "Dinner served at 8." If your party is more flexible, expect people to show up on the later side of the evening—so you may want to crank up your opening hour a little bit earlier. If you don't put a finish date on the evening, expect people to stay later and expect some dinner or heartier fare than a baked brie wheel. If you start your party after 9, you're clear of dinner. Just plan on having snacks and sweets.

- **Address.** Consider providing driving instructions and any special parking information for your guests.

- **Instructions for RSVP**. Include your phone number, email, and the reply-before date. If you're planning a large party, do not put "RSVP" on your invitations unless you really want to get a million phone calls or emails. Instead, make things easy on yourself and say "Regrets Only" so that only the people who cannot attend will contact you.

- **Theme info.** Include dress or costume suggestions.

No matter what you end up doing, make sure you notify your guests about your intended party with some panache. Visit a stationery store or explore the Internet, because there are tons of cute options that you can personalize easily at home with your own printer. You can even go as basic as a flyer and use a photocopier as your friend. Have friends who are incessantly doodling? Put their talents to good use and have them decorate your invitation.

It's always fun to start off an invitation with a catchy little hook. Here are some suggestions:

BBQ/Dinner Party
Where's the beef? It's at _____'s house. Join us for a BBQ to celebrate _____.

The Sexy Bitch's Party

Bridal Shower (lingerie theme)

I see London, I see France, Let's see _____'s underpants! Join us for a lingerie shower celebrating the upcoming marriage of _____.

Halloween

Turn a trick, get a treat! Come over for _____'s Halloween party!

TOP 10 THINGS FOR A PARTYING SEXY BITCH TO DO BEFORE SHE DIES

1. Attend Mardi Gras and drink Hurricanes all night on Bourbon Street.
2. Hit the autobahn for a fast ride to Oktoberfest in Munich, Germany and see what German dudes wear under their lederhosen.
3. Vegas, baby. Vegas.
4. Skinny dip often.
5. Drink a flute of fine champagne with a delicious morsel of a man in the moonlit shadow of the Eiffel Tower.
6. Enjoy a cozy hot tub with a hunkalicious movie star (okay, even a movie extra counts).
7. Get close to a legendary sexy bitch and snag a front row seat to a Madonna concert.
8. Crash a fancy wedding and kiss the best man.
9. Rent a convertible for the day and cruise Highway 101 on the California Coast.
10. Practice your Italian and take in the sun while you wine taste at the many vineyards that dot the Tuscan countryside.

part three

throwing the party

Hopefully you've moved beyond the antics of your youth to embrace festive options that do not involve playing Donkey Kong in a fraternity house by rolling empty keg containers down the stairs. The goal of hosting parties is to have a great time with minimal minutes spent wearing an apron and consulting recipes. Put your time toward thinking of creative ways to celebrate and make people comfortable rather than planning the intricacies of a seven-course meal. After all, it is much more fun to daydream about our guest list and to plan ways to entertain our friends than it is to assemble a shopping list that includes 158 ingredients.

Since this book is all about saving you time and headache, I have assembled party ideas from my entourage of "experts" (they also double as my friends) so that you can start whipping together some days and evenings of delight. Of course, feel free to modify these concepts to fit your lifestyle and interests. So sit back and enjoy the following ideas from what I like to think of as a greatest hits party collection…

10 goosing the classics: party all year long

So birthday and holiday parties are the oldest ones in the book, right? True, but that doesn't mean that they're totally played out. Some of these classic parties are classics for a reason. Who doesn't love having a birthday party thrown for them? And it's not just birthdays that can be made more original; try putting some new spin on those rather played-out holiday parties. Yes, you can play it safe and stick with a traditional gift exchange for a Christmas party, or you can get a little naughty and steal gifts from your friends instead. So let's explore our options, shall we?

anytime: birthday party

All of the etiquette books say it's uncouth to throw a birthday party for yourself, but we know that's one of those good old rules that was meant to be broken. You know what you want so you should go out and set it up so things can be exactly the way you want them to be. If you are still feeling a little too modest to toot your own horn and host a party honoring your fine self, get some friends to host it for you and simply use them as puppets. Remember the man behind the curtain in *The Wizard of Oz*? Okay, so he was old and had a receding hairline but you get the picture, right? YOU are the person calling all of the shots here just like the dude behind the curtain in Oz. If you are really bold, you can even stage a surprise party and feign shock that all of your thoughtful friends wanted to surprise you on this special day but let's keep things simple for now…

First of all, the focus at this party is on you and only you. Marvelous, sexy pictures of you should decorate every nook and cranny of this shindig. These pictures should highlight all of your major life accomplishments so far. If you are concerned that there are not enough tremendous moments, that's okay because you can always stage a few. The wonders of digital photography never cease; now you can be seen standing on the gold medal podium at the Olympics accepting the highest honors for your accomplishments in figure skating, you can be hugged by your dearest friend Jennifer Lopez after winning Best New Vocalist at the MTV Music Awards, you can be discussing your latest bestselling novel with Katie Couric on the "Today Show," and you can be enjoying a lazy afternoon on a sailboat in the Greek Isles with your ex-boyfriend Brad Pitt (you broke up with him, of course). Sure, some of your friends may be surprised that they never knew some of these things about you but that's okay: you're a sexy bitch and don't need to explain yourself to anyone. Note to [your]self: you should probably buy a digital camera, a Photoshop kit, and some celebrity magazines with that birthday check that your grandmother sent so that you can get your life story together.

You should also wear a crown that is dazzling with bling and a boa that makes you look like you just left the set of the movie that you're starring in with George Clooney. Since it is your birthday, earlier in the day you should have indulged in a relaxing spa and shopping day. I would advise you to skip any facials though because they can leave your complexion blotchy and blemished temporarily. So, stick with a new haircut and color, massage, manicure, and pedicure. Hopefully in your shopping excursion you found something that makes you look vibrant and voluptuous in all of the right places. Wear it.

As for presents, yes, you could be altruistic and tell people in the invitation to donate to a humanitarian cause that you cherish, but who are we kidding? We all know that the cause nearest and dearest to your heart is YOU. So, don't kid yourself or anyone else and just come right out with it. You can even register for your birthday at many fine shops. Or write on the invitation that you prefer diamonds over pearls, convertible sports cars over sporting equipment, and cash is always welcomed. Everyone appreciates an honest friend.

When it comes to food, I do not recommend cooking for your own birthday party because it's just way too much work for crying out loud. Order in food or have your party catered. Better yet, have friends take you out for dinner before the party. Yes, you should have cake and lots of it. Cupcakes have been trendy lately and I think that they're adorable so feel free to deviate from the typical birthday cake and go with little sweetly (or naughtily) decorated cupcakes instead. If you do end up making these yourself, eat plenty of frosting and use a mix because they're easy and fairly foolproof. Incidentally, all diets are suspended on birthdays. I think it's in the Constitution somewhere. Note: if you have a legalistic mind, you would know that EVERY day is someone's birthday so you can always have an excuse to splurge—hooray!

As an icebreaker and conversation starter, make stickers for your guests that show basic horoscope information. Simply buy blank name tags at the drugstore or use big mailing stickers and print them out from your computer. Horoscope information can easily be found on the Internet. You will want to include horoscope sign, compatible signs, signs to avoid, basic characteristics of this sign, some celebrities who share this sign, and some horoscope information for this sign. Get creative and make the horoscopes sexy so that everyone will be plotting their next romantic move all evening.

January: new year's eve party

Grab your noisemakers and get ready to bring in the New Year... again, and again next year, and again the following year, and so on. Yeah, really it's kind of surprising that New Year's Eve gets so much attention because it never really changes much. Everyone grabs their bottle of champagne, watches fireworks live or on TV, and usually spends way too much money on an overpriced party ticket or *prix fixe* dinner. Oy. How can we liven up this holiday that really doesn't have anything remotely "New" about it?

Going out is always an option but it is a surefire way to sink a ton of cash quickly. Tough way to kick off that resolution about watching your budget, eh? My suggestion is to host a party. First of all, you won't have to risk cruising the roads on a night where many drivers have been drinking without thinking. Second, you can invite all of your best buddies over and see where things lead. Seems like an easy party: get some champagne, turn up the music, and put up some decorations. Easy. Well, it can be as easy as this or you can make things a little more interesting. First of all, every guest should make an Evening's Resolution as soon as they walk in the door. Yup, they must make a goal for the night and do everything within their power to make it happen. The zanier the resolution, the better. For example, your resolution could be to shave a man's leg. You'll have all kinds of interesting discussions with various fellows throughout the party as you attempt to locate someone to accommodate your vision. If you play your cards right, you'll get to take off a dude's pants and see where things lead. Just be careful with that razor lying around. Of course, if he's going to help you, you better reciprocate. Who knows what kind of crazy idea he's got? Hmmm.

Alright, let's get our minds out of the gutter and return to party planning. The other fun thing you could add to your party is to have a fortune teller at the party so that they can provide predictions on the upcoming year. No, you do not need to go out and hire Lida the Seer from the creepy street corner by the wig shop; make life easy and convince a friend that it will be a fun gig for the evening. Try to choose a friend who is creative and tends to have some wild ideas. She should try to work sex into all of the horoscopes to keep people entertained. She should dress up with eccentric jewelry, a turban, and too much makeup. You can go to a gardening store and pick up one of those things that people stick in their backyards that look like crystal balls. Or you could have your fortune teller read tea leaves. This is really easy. Just go and buy some loose tea, boil it, and have the fortune teller pour cup after cup of tea and gaze into it while making up some wild predictions. The last option of course is to have her use tarot cards and make up predictions. Or if you are really putting all of this together last minute, just use regular playing cards. All props aside, the secret is in the predictions. If you have a fortune teller who can make people laugh, use astrological jargon, and come up with some zany ideas, your friends will love you. Incidentally, I would make sure to keep your seer soaked in libations all night so her "second sight" will be unleashed.

Sample fortune teller line:

Ahhh, yes, as Mercury moves into the second house, you will find yourself cleaning a camel with a red-headed man who wears an eye patch. Beware of kicking camels.

tips for tea leaf reading

- Use a shallow but wide white mug.
- The person having a fortune read should drink the tea until about one teaspoonful of tea remains in the mug.
- Tea leaves near the top represent things that will happen soon; leaves directly beneath the handle indicate present and immediate happenings; leaves on the sides of the mug denote more distant events; leaves at the bottom mean that something is very far away and possibly unlikely to happen.
- When trying to "read" the tea leaves, stare at the remnants long enough to blur your vision so that you start seeing images. Once you think you see "a flower" or "a cat" it's up to your imagination to start concocting what this means.

There is absolutely nothing scientific to these instructions, nor are these based on any real professional advice. My friends and I constructed this after lacing tea with various liquors. Best bets for most imaginative results: green tea and rum, or Irish tea (black tea with whiskey). See what works for you and your seer.

tips for telling fortunes with regular playing cards

• Create a pre-determined general code for reading cards and stick with it so you don't get stuck when trying to make up a fortune. You can also search online for many different card coding systems.

• The basic system is to choose what each suit represents. For example: hearts can represent love, diamonds represent money, etc.

• Next figure out a basic cue for each number. For example: a two symbolizes that someone else is about to join your life, three can be something bad is going to happen, four could be a new sexual position may enter your life, etc.

• Have a fancy shuffling technique and figure out how you will want to arrange your cards in advance so that you look appear smooth and professional.

february: valentine's day

You either love this holiday or you hate it depending on your romantic situation as February 14th approaches. We can all agree that it is the corniest holiday, but do you approach it as if you were walking to your execution, do you put up with the cheesiness and have fun with it, or do you drape yourself in doilies and red satin and prance around the neighborhood leaving chocolates on everyone's doorstep? If the last description is you, then I must seriously question why you are even reading this book to start with, so let's assume that you fall into one of the first two categories depending on your mood and love situation. Either way you look at it, you can have a good time on Valentine's Day without having to grab a bow and arrow and shoot every cupid that you see in store windows. I mean you could hide out at home and share a pint of ice cream with your cat and feel sorry for yourself but this is bound to put you on track to Loserville with a one-way ticket. No way, babe! You are too fabulous to be found pining away in the spinster section of your nearby library. Stick with me here as I outline the two approaches to Valentine's Day that are guaranteed to keep you more sexy and bitchier than ever.

the "venus doesn't need a penis" approach to valentine's day

As you can probably infer from the name of this approach, you don't need a date to paaarty and have a good time on February 14th. What you do need is a sense of humor. There are a couple of things you can do here. You can either get a bunch of your sexy bitch friends together, go out, and hit your local version of the Golden Banana and watch men (usually gay) strut their stuff and strip for your edification, or you can host a party of your own.

If you're going out, focus on having dinner and drinks at a lively, funky place where you and your bitches will not be surrounded by swooning couples gazing adoringly into each other's eyes. That's right, avoid all romantic getaways. But don't worry, this doesn't leave you stuck at Pizza Palace munching on pepperoni slices either. You should look for a place that has dancing, loud music, a fully stocked bar, and spicy food so that you can keep your heart pumping and thumping with good times into the wee hours of the morning. Men who are easy on the eyes are also quite welcome during a bitches' night out, so factor that into your search for just the right place for your evening.

If you decide to host an anti-romantic party at your place, prepare to tie one on. First of all, send out invitations to single people only. Couples will only rile your nerves and make everyone feel uncomfortable. You can try to make this a match-making event, but this is kind of a high pressure night to get anything reliable to stick. So, simply plan on getting some good friends together for a night of debauchery.

Guests should be encouraged to wear only black. Anyone who shows up wearing anything with a heart or with red or pink will pay the penalty of wearing a cheesehead hat, or other suitably unromantic headgear, on their head all night. As guests approach your anti-love lair, they should be greeted with a banner that reads "Cupid is Stupid" or something of that ilk so that the vibe of this party is felt immediately. Your pad should be decorated with pictures of famous celebrity pairings that have headed to Splitsville, so that everyone can bask in the misfortune of people who appear to have it all. Call this your "Wall of Sizzled Flame."

Some famous couples who have broken up are:

Brad Pitt & Jennifer Anniston

J. Lo & lotsa dudes, inc. Ben Affleck

Julia Roberts & Lyle Lovett

Madonna & Sean Penn

Donald & Ivana Trump

You can also revel in everyone's romantic distress by having guests enter a Worst Break-Up Contest. Have guests write down a description of their worst break up and drop it into a goldfish bowl (preferably empty of fish) or a bowl or something, along with a dollar (or so). After everyone appears to have had enough to eat and drink and is pretty boisterous, read the top contenders aloud and have everyone vote on the winner. When the winner is announced, they win everyone's sympathy and some cash. If you're planning ahead, you can even reward your winner with a gift certificate to a local sex toy store or buy something cheesy and funny. Everyone loves turning a loser into a winner, so have some fun and get into the spirit with turning a terrible experience into something terrific.

the slightly rosier approach to valentine's day

I should caution you that if you embrace this approach you must still try to keep your feet on the ground and stay suitably cynical toward this holiday. Puh-lease do not go overboard and start decorating your party with posters of kittens and puppies rolling around in roses and by all means, do not break out any annoying Anne Geddes pictures. Ugh. Roly poly babies decorated in flowers are enough to make anyone flee a party upon first sight, so throw anything like that away now!

Okay, now that we know where we stand, let's review this approach: your mission is to host a party that gets into the spirit of romance yet doesn't make anyone feel nauseous. You could decide to go with a theme. For example, guests could dress as famous pairs. This theme works well for large gatherings because it is not limited to couples. For example, friends or couples can dress up like salt and pepper, night and day, good and evil, or heaven and earth. And, of course, there are endless possibilities for famous couples, both romantic and platonic: Adam and Eve, Sonny and Cher, Cheech and Chong, Doublemint Twins, Batman and Robin, and on and on.

Another theme would be throwing a lingerie party, where the guests wear only their skivvies. This requires a daring streak in your guests, but I'm sure they'll rise to the occasion. Promise plenty of libations and your guests will be happy to cut to the chase and show everyone what they're made of. Upon arrival, everyone can be given a porn name. For this nifty party trick, guests take the name of their first pet and add the name of a street on which they have lived. Voila, suddenly you go from having a party filled with boring old Dick and Janes to having Pepper Jones, Princess Blossom, and Dozer Denny. Don't forget name tags so that everyone can sport their new name for all to see!

To help catch the love bug, go out and purchase some little brown lunch bags and cheapo drugstore valentines like you used to send as a little kid. As you set up for your soiree, you will create a station to make valentines. Put those bags out with markers, glitter, stickers and any other silly decorating materials, along with the valentines, out on a table and encourage guests to make a little baggie for themselves and to fill out valentines and "mail" them to someone else's baggie. By the end of the night, everyone should be feeling loved because of all of the nickel valentines they received.

When guests arrive, give them a ticket that they can fill out and drop into a bowl for a raffle at the end of the evening. As the night progresses, you can announce winners from your raffle and award them with romantic and kinky gifts, such as chocolate body paint, massage oils, colorful flavored condoms, and other funny little sexy gifts. Ooh la la!

Serve snacks at this party and try to make everything heart-shaped. Amaze your guests with your ingenuity on this one. With kitchen scissors, cut up tortillas into heart shapes and make quesadillas. You should also have lots of chocolate at this party, and I mean LOTS. I'm talking about candy chocolates to brownies to a heart-shaped cake covered in chocolate frosting. You can easily make a heart-shaped cake by buying a cake mix and using a square pan and a circular pan. Whip up the batter, bake it in both cake pans, cool them and cut the circular cake into halves and attach them to the square cake. Smother the whole thing in chocolate frosting and prepare to dig in. Strawberries dipped in chocolate are also a tasty treat and easy to make. Yum.

february/march: mardi gras madness

Looking for an easy way to hit the Big Easy for one of the most famous parties in the world? Good news: you don't need to hoof it all the way to New Orleans; you can host a Mardi Gras bash at your own pad, complete with beads, boys, and bedlam. Depending on the year, Mardi Gras happens anytime from mid-February to early March, so it's the perfect way to keep the winter blues at bay. Check the Internet to find out when "Fat Tuesday" falls this year to time your invitations just right.

The key ingredient to any Mardi Gras festivity is wild revelry, but you also need some good food, decorations, dancing music, and munchies. Let's start with decorations, shall we? Green, gold, and purple are the official colors of Mardi Gras so you need to go hog wild digging up anything you can in those colors: tulle, balloons, colored paper, bras, panties, and boxers. What's going on with the undies? Mardi Gras parades are a time in your life when it is perfectly acceptable—even expected—for you to throw your inhibitions to the wind…along with your bra! That's right, get everyone in the mood by decorating your party place with these critical party accessories. You may even want to find some pictures of New Orleans and decorate with homemade street signs for famous New Orleans landmarks, such as Bourbon Street, The French Quarter, and The Garden District. Mardi Gras is a time for masking, so tell your guests to bring one. And stock up on as many plastic Mardi Gras beads as possible. Guests should be covered in them by the end of the night. Traditionally the beads are thrown off the parade floats at women who lift their shirts and men who drop their trousers!

Next we need some good tunes. Look for zydeco, jazz, or any good blues music to liven up your party with authentic sound.

Since the emphasis on this holiday is on partying and not slaving in the kitchen, the menu needs to be easy. I recommend going to the grocery store to load up on Cajun spices and barbequing steaks, chicken, and shrimps so you cut down on dishes and hassle. Be sure to serve the food in fairly small pieces, because you don't want guests to be sitting down with plates and flatware when they should be up on their feet dancing! You'll also need a King Cake. Traditionally these cakes are some sort of jelly roll with a plastic baby baked inside. Whoever finds the baby in his or her cake slice wins a prize. Rather than mustering the effort to create this authentic cake, I would simply buy a tasty cake, lift it carefully with a spatula, and jam a plastic baby into the bottom of it for someone to find. After all, it's the spirit that counts!

Obviously beverages are also critical to this event. Stock up on the usual beer, wine, and liquor, but also go for a drink that is indigenous to New Orleans…the Hurricane!

hurricane cocktail

1 oz. white rum
1 oz. Jamaican dark rum
1 oz. Bacardi 151 rum
3 oz. orange juice
3 oz. pineapple juice (unsweetened)
1/2 oz. grenadine syrup
crushed ice

Steps:
Mix all ingredients well and serve in a hurricane glass with a fruit garnish—an orange wedge or something comparable.

march: kiss me, i'm irish st. patrick's day party

Okay, so you don't need to be Irish to get kissed at this party, but you do need to feel the sassy lassie spirit to get lucky. Everyone loves the opportunity to don their green clothes and get wild. In fact, EVERY-THING needs to be green (and wild) for this party. Find green balloons, Christmas lights, paper, tablecloths, and anything else that could possibly be green.

Serve a potato bar. This is an easy (and cheap) party dish. Just make a bunch of baked potatoes and provide garnishes so that everyone can dress up their own jacket potato with toppings that look good to them. Include bacon bits, butter, sour cream, chives, melted cheddar cheese (keep it warm in a small fondue pot or butter warmer), chopped green onions, broccoli, bean chili, mustard, ranch dressing, cilantro, mushrooms, and other good stuff.

Also set out some green M&Ms and Lucky Charms cereal. For a fun dessert, make Lucky Charms treats (Rice Krispies treats with a twist) using the recipe below. Have lots of beer on hand, including some Guinness. Lighter beers can be made green easily with a splash of green food coloring.

Lucky Charms Treats

1/4 cup butter
10 oz. marshmallows
6 cups Lucky Charms

Steps:
1. Melt butter in saucepan over low heat and add in marshmallows until melted and creamy.
2. Remove from heat and stir in Lucky Charms until all of the cereal pieces are well coated.
3. Using greased spoon, press mixture into a greased 9x13-inch baking pan.
4. Cut into squares when completely cool.

limerick contest

Limericks get their name from a city in Ireland, and they're silly (often raunchy) little poems with an easy formula to follow: They're five lines long and usually have a *duh-duh-DA* rhythm, with two little beats and a downbeat. (That's called anapest, for all you literary pests out there. Don't get too hung up on the rhythm, though: it's basically a free-for-all.)

The first two lines and the last one all have three downbeats (*duh-duh-DA-duh-duh-DA-duh-duh-DA*), and their last words should all rhyme.

The third and fourth lines are shorter, with only two downbeats (*duh-duh-DA-duh-duh-DA*), and their last words should rhyme with each other.

But telling you about limericks is like using a diagram to teach someone how to have a roll in the hay—the learning is in the doing. Here's an example:

There once were some fine sexy bitches
Who threw parties without any glitches.
They were brimming with sass
And liked shaking that ass
Till the guys were all popping their britches.

Okay, so this is pretty tame but you get the idea of where this limerick thing is going. Preferably, guests should be encouraged to err on the side of raunchy. Have a prize for the winner of the contest or you can go with multiple categories and have several winners. (funniest, dirtiest, worst rhyme...)

Oh, and last but not least, don't forget the green jelly shots! Follow the directions on the green gelatin box but use alcohol (vodka, rum, whatever) where it says to use cold water. Pour into little paper cups to set—guests squeeze the cups into their mouths to "drink" the shots. May the sun shine warm on your face, may the wind be at your back, and may the road rise to meet you...but not because you're passing out in the gutter.

may: cinco de mayo

This Mexican-themed fiesta is a must because it's easy, fun, and encourages people to wear sombreros. Mexican food is a snap to prepare and it's cheap, which is also good. Costco and other markets have plenty of tasty frozen and prepared Mexican foods, such as taquitos and quesadillas. Obviously chips with assorted salsas, dips, and guacamole are always a hit. Make sure you locate some mariachi music and a piñata that is filled with candy, condoms, or whatever else will make your friends dive for the floor and squeal like kindergartners. Serve Mexican beers and Olivier's World Famous Margarita recipe, and I guarantee that the fiesta will be a hit.

Olivier's World Famous Margaritas

1 can of limeade (found in the frozen section of your grocery store)
3 oz. Triple Sec (or to taste)
6 oz. tequila (or to taste)
1 bottle of a light beer (a Corona works perfectly)
1 lime
rock salt
ice

The Sexy Bitch's Party

Steps:

In a blender mix the limeade with all of the alcohol and ice. You might be wondering what the beer is for: it gives the margaritas a nice foamy quality, which is very festive. Slice up the lime as garnish and you can use the rock salt around the rim of the glasses. If you make these *muy* strong, you may find yourself speaking in tongues. *Arriba, arriba!*

Mexican Cups

These mini scoops are tasty and easy to whip up.

1 or 2 mini muffin tins
won-ton wrappers (from the refrigerated section of your super-
    market)
Monterey Jack cheese
Possible toppings include: salsa, guacamole, sour cream, and
    refried beans

Steps:
1. Fill each muffin hole with a won-ton wrapper so they're
   shaped like mini taco salad shell bowls.
2. Slice up cubes of cheese and pop them into the wrappers.
3. Cook at 375°F for 8-11 minutes.
4. Serve on plate with suggested toppings available for
   scooping.
5. Dig in!

GOOSING THE CLASSICS

Easy Homemade Salsa

This salsa is pureed instead of diced, making it a cinch.

5 fresh tomatoes coarsely chopped
1 medium onion coarsely chopped
5 jalapenos chopped
1 bunch fresh cilantro chopped
1/4 cup rice wine vinegar
juice of one lime
1 tsp. salt

Mix all ingredients together and puree with hand blender or regular blender until it is a consistency that looks and tastes *muy bueno!*

Mexican Casserole

This dish is a snap to put together well in advance of your fiesta, and the leftovers are perfect hangover food. Buy a rotisserie chicken already cooked from your supermarket to really make this a breeze (often these are even cheaper than buying uncooked chicken breasts).

16 oz. can whole kernel corn, drained
16 oz. can black beans (rinsed and drained) or refried beans
    (whichever you prefer)
10 oz. can of tomatoes and green chilis
8 oz. container of sour cream
8 oz. jar of picante sauce
2 cups of shredded cheddar cheese
2 cups cooked rice
2 cups shredded or cubed cooked chicken meat
1/4 tsp. freshly ground black pepper

6 green onions, chopped
sliced black olives for sprinkling on top
2 cups shredded Monterey Jack cheese

Steps:
1. Preheat oven to 350°F.
2. Combine corn, beans, tomatoes, chilis, sour cream, picante
   sauce, cheddar cheese, rice, chicken, and pepper. Spoon into a
   lightly greased, 9x13-inch baking dish.
3. Sprinkle with onions, olives, and Monterey Jack cheese.
4. Bake for 50 minutes.

Sangria

This recipe is perfect for a Cinco de Mayo fiesta—olé!

1/2 cup dark rum
bottle red wine (Zinfandel, Chianti)
1/2 cup Triple Sec
2 Tbs. sugar
2 oranges (one sliced into rounds, the second sliced into
     wedges for garnish)
lime sliced into rounds
lemon sliced into rounds
apple sliced into wedges
2 cups Club Soda

Mix all ingredients and serve over ice garnished with orange
wedge. It tastes even better if you let it sit in the refrigerator for
a few hours.

july: bastille day

The first rule for a French theme party: no berets. After this rule, there aren't many. The French are fabulous at knowing how to indulge with decadent foods, rich wines, and witty repartee. Don't forget the French mean business when they party; they invented the ménage à trois!

Decor should be red, white, and blue, just like the elegantly simple French flag. You can go bistro style and incorporate red-and-white-checked tablecloths, or go with more of a South of France palette and snag some Provence-patterned napkins and table coverings. Find some fun little Eiffel Tower-decorated things to sprinkle around your *maison*, and voila!

Your menu should be French-inspired. Where do you start? Fondue! It has come a long way, baby. You no longer have to nibble on pieces of bread that looked like they've been dipped in Cheez Whiz. You can create a broth base and dip pieces of raw meat (just be careful to follow the cookbook directions and handle the meat correctly so you don't send your guests home with a case of salmonella). In addition, you should have some tasty red wines, champagne, and Perrier water.

Put together a *"fromage"* (that means cheese!) plate to be truly authentic. If you're really trying to be the real thing, serve it as a dessert and include a mixtures of hard cheeses, soft cheeses, and fruit. Just don't pre-cut the cheese into slices—*mon dieu!* Serve the mildest cheese first, then move on to stinkier and stinkier ones. Many grocery stores have wonderful cheese departments where they welcome questions and would be happy to assist your construction of a *très bien* cheese plate. Also try farmer's markets for tasty selections of local organic cheeses. Yum!

Mild cheeses: Brie, Terroir, Neufchatel

Strong: Muenster, Roquefort, Camembert, Raclette

French Onion Soup

This is a tasty and easy soup to make, but since you make each portion in an individual bowl, it is best made for an intimate tête à tête!

2 Tbs. olive oil
1 Tbs. butter
2 large onions sliced
2 bay leaves
1 tsp. thyme
1 tsp. flour
1/4 cup sherry
3 cups beef broth
1 cup water
1 cup shredded Gruyère cheese
toasted bread rounds

Steps:
1. Heat oil and butter, add sliced onions and sauté until wilted about 10-15 minutes.
2. Add sherry and sauté for another 5 minutes.
3. Add bay leaves, thyme and flour. Cook for approximately 5 minutes.
4. Add beef broth and water and let simmer for about 30 minutes.

5. When serving, pour hot soup into ovenproof bowls, place toasted bread rounds on top of soup and sprinkle with shredded Gruyère.

6. Broil until cheese is bubbly and just starting to brown.

A party like this can be whipped together at any time of year, but don't forget that July 13th is Bastille Day, France's version of the Fourth of July. So, get out the wine and prepare to "let them eat cake."

Plus, this is always a great excuse to do a lot of French kissing!

october: "turn a trick, get a treat" party

Give everyone a treat and host a Halloween party. Of course, this is a dress-up party, so you must award costume prizes to the Funniest, Scariest, Grossest, Most Tasteless, Most Creative, Best Couple's Costume, and Best Group Costume. When you're creating your invitations, make sure you tell your invitees that awards will be handed out and tell them the categories in advance so that they can work on raising the bar of the costume quality. As the host, you need to have a killer costume so that you can show everyone how it is done. No pressure, of course. Trawl the news headlines and cheesy celebrity magazines when you're in line at the grocery store and see if you can come up with a timely *au courant* costume that will leave your guests buzzing. If you're willing to drop some serious cash on this endeavor, visit a local costume shop and survey the possibilities.

Candy is a must, so load up bowls of candy and leave them wherever there is room—your friends will be wired on sugar all night. Capitalize on Halloween's campy spirit and serve s'mores by either using fondue pots (one for marshmallow and one for chocolate) or set up a bonfire somewhere outside (yeah, not a good idea to set one on the porch of a neighbor who you don't like).

Decorating your lair of love is also a great idea on the scariest night of the year. If you can do the haunted house thang, I highly encourage you to go for it. Here are a few easy ways:

- Buy batting (also known as quilt stuffing) from a local fabric store and give your furniture the cobweb look.
- Use colored lighting to create creepy effects.
- Scary music and recorded screams set a relaxing tone for your guests (ha!).
- Go to a dollar store and buy lots of little plastic bugs that can appear to be infesting the party.
- Peeled grapes, gummy worms and gelatin constitute an excellent guts bowl.
- Create a bubbling, bloody cauldron by boiling tomato soup on your stovetop.
- Design ghosts by covering balloons with white sheets. Use the balloon as the head and let it drift around the room eerily. Helium balloons work best for this trick.

Key props around the house should include a Ouija board. Another little mean-spirited game that you and your friends can play is making tombstones for people that you know but wish you didn't. Cut out gray tombstone-shaped pieces of construction paper and leave out markers for people to write epitaphs for your dearly despised. Oh, and bobbing for apples is always an entertaining way for everyone to humiliate themselves.

december: christmas party

Have you been naughty or nice? Forget the nice—only the naughty need attend this Christmas party!

Spare everyone the agony of having to attend their lame office holiday party and give them some festive cheer to get them through the next year. Sure, deck the halls with holly and evergreen, but make sure you smother your party palace in mistletoe so that kissing is *de rigueur* for the evening! Buy white lights and cover every surface to create a romantic glow.

Play a game called Murder with your guests. On your invitation, instruct everyone to bring a gift that cost less than $20. As guests arrive, place gifts in a pile that's easy to get to later. Once everyone seems sufficiently rambunctious, get the game going. Start off by having everyone pick a number—one through however many guests you have. Number 1 gets to choose any gift and open it. Hopefully it's something he really likes and becomes instantly attached to, because number 2 gets to open a gift of her choosing. If she likes what Number 1 got better, she can switch with no questions asked. In case you haven't figured this out, Number 1 is going to get robbed all night of anything cool that he happens to open. If you don't want the game to last forever, limit the number of switches that can happen in one turn. So, if Number 16 opens up a set of coffee mugs designed to look like bowling ball pins, she can turn around and steal the nifty martini set that Number 11 opened, forcing Number 11 to open something that has not been opened yet. Needless to say, higher numbers are desirable, and it's also fun to bring some hokey thing that no one is going to want and is going to be traded more times than a baseball player with one arm.

Another fun thing to do at a Christmas party is to make and decorate gingerbread mansions. Get some magazines that feature cribs of the rich and famous to inspire your group of architects and decorators. Along with slabs of gingerbread that can be sliced and diced to fit the keen eye of your builders, include plenty of candy to serve as special architectural intricacies.

11 hot and themey: theme parties

The number-one cause of party burnout (according to my highly scientific study) is same old, same old. If it's Tuesday, this must be happy hour at O'Pootertoot's, and if it's Saturday, this must be Marisa's place for screwdrivers and the same mp3 playlist you've danced to a million times. You must fight party conformity with every inch of your being, and a theme party is just the weapon you need. If you're planning a bender, give your friends something unusual to look forward to—throw a dress-like-your-favorite-dead-person party, have a gamelan dance-a-thon, or hold a Himalayan night with food from your local Tibetan restaurant and a live yak. (It could happen!) Here are some ideas for keeping your parties from having that not-so-fresh feeling.

"tulle-y" a night to remember: the prom

Throwing a prom is a riot; there's nothing like encouraging your friends to relive a moment of their teenage years. Either rent a low-budget space, such as a community center or another locale that will seem charmingly high-schoolish, or host it at your place. Send out invitations and encourage your friends to visit thrift stores to locate retro dresses that will take you right back to the era of your youth. Ask guests to bring their old prom pictures and tack these to the wall so everyone can enjoy a blast from the past. Cover the party space in streamers, get a bunch of CDs with music from those years, and cajole a friend into setting up a "Prom Picture" corner where couples can be photographed. Be sure to stir things up with a rousing game of spin the bottle and clearly label a "Makeout Corner."

Tip: It is imperative that you crown a prom king and queen. Other possible prizes include: Biggest Hair, Most Colorful Tux, and Most Likely to Be an Extra in the Remake of *Sixteen Candles*.

For this type of party, you will want to have a table of easy appetizers to keep the munchies at bay.

Baked Brie

1 wheel brie cheese (any size depending on number of guests)
1 jar pineapple/apricot preserves or chutney
Slivered almonds

Steps:
1. Top brie with apricot/pineapple preserves and almonds.
2. Bake at 300°F for approximately 15 minutes.
Serve with an assortment of crackers.

Grilled Seasonal Fruits
Wrapped with Prosciutto

prosciutto
seasonal fruits (such as fig, apple, melon, pear, peach, nectarine)

Steps:
1. Slice fruit into bite-size pieces and wrap with prosciutto, then place on a skewer.
2. Grill over medium heat until prosciutto starts to brown.

the croquet social

Throw an afternoon lawn party featuring croquet or any sort of garden game: bocce, badminton, horse shoes, tennis, you name it. Invite everyone to arrive for an afternoon's worth of sporting, replete in their garden party ensembles: hats, whites, oxfords, and any other preppy attire they can dream up.

Gin and Tonic

Take highball glass, insert ice cubes, insert gin, insert tonic.
That's it, Muffy.

dance party

This theme can go in a million different directions, based on your interests. You can go out to a place that offers dance lessons, or you can find a private instructor who can come to your house. You can go old school and learn how to foxtrot and prance around with classic moves, or you can go a little more current and try swing, hip-hop, or salsa. Grab your partner and plan a square dancing party if you're feeling wild. And last but not least, don't be afraid of hula dancing or belly dancing if you want to try something fun and unique.

say "I do" to coming to my party: it's a wedding!

Let me clarify: this is NOT a real wedding, with caterers and mothers-in-law. If your set has embarked on the marriage circuit, everyone has a closet full of hideous bridesmaid dresses they're unlikely to wear a second time—and many have wedding dresses they only got to wear once but wish they could again. Well, here's their chance. At this party everyone should come wearing their own wedding attire, their most atrocious bridesmaid dress, or their swankiest tux. If nobody's anywhere near getting married, hit the thrift shops and live the fantasy—or the nightmare, depending on your perspective.

Decorate with a few bouquets of flowers and make sure you serve some champagne drinks, take photos, and give prizes such as Most Experienced Bridesmaid/Bridegroom, Hates the Very Idea of Getting Married, Married the Longest, Married Most Recently, Cake Fell Over at the Wedding, Worst Wedding Picture…you get the idea.

If you and your friends feel really generous and spontaneous, you could get everyone to chip in to send someone to a fancy hotel at the end of the night. Just have everyone kick in some dough when they arrive and have them collect a number. At a certain time of the evening, do a drawing and send the lucky winner off to enjoy the night in a ritzy pad. Obviously, indicate that you are going to do this on the invitation and instruct everyone to show up with an overnight bag.

Serve a variety of appetizers so that you can avoid seating all of these brides and their puffy skirts. Have some chairs and stools sprinkled around, but keep your guests circulating. Put together a table full of tasty treats. Serve a wedding cake too of course!

Salmon Dill Dip with Caviar Garnish

1 lb. smoked salmon
1 cup whipped cream cheese
1/4 cup Parmesan cheese
2 tsp. dill
1 tsp. garlic powder
dash Tabasco
dash white pepper
chopped parsley and caviar garnish

Mix together and serve with sliced baguette.

tasting sampler party

This is a versatile party idea that can be applied to anything that you enjoy eating or drinking multiples of. You can create wine flights and serve wines from all over the world, or many from a certain region, or have people bring their favorite cheap wine and do taste tests. For example, you could do a wine flight from South America. There's a great variety of good and pretty inexpensive wines hailing from the southern hemisphere. Look for wines from Chile and Argentina, including chardonnays, merlots, etc. The same can be done with beers, teas (host a tea party!), coffees, and anything else you can think of.

get the band back together party

Abba, Sonny & Cher, Michael Jackson… the costume ideas are endless for this rock star party. Everyone must glam up and come on over for some karaoke. Decorate your pad with pics of famous rockers through the ages and get your sound system jamming.

You can even have a karaoke contest a la "American Idol" and have a battle of the amateur bands with a couple of friends as judges.

One warning: to prevent "death by karaoke," have mercy on your guests and make sure you set up the sound system in a space that is escapable. Believe it or not, some guests may need to take a break from the tunes from time to time.

oscar party

Hollywood's biggest night can become your big night too if you throw an Oscar bash. This is a formal affair, and everyone should show up in all their finery. Decorate the party spot with Oscars pictures from past celebrity magazines and try to incorporate as much of a Hollywood motif as possible—roll out a red carpet from a party store, make palm trees out of paper, and cut out stars with your friends' names on them, then tape them to the floor to create your own Walk of Stars.

You should definitely have an Oscar pool: nothing like a little monetary incentive to hold people's interest when the awards broadcast lags. Choose the most obvious categories, such as Best Picture, Best Actor, Best Actress, etc. and print up ballots. Usually you can find pre-made ballots online at sites like www.oscar.com. Ask everyone to put $5 into the kitty, and have a pool for people to win if they choose all of the winners on their ballot. You can also make up your own categories: hottest man, most romantic, most cheesy, best kiss, etc. and have people vote for this too.

oscar trivia game

Find out whether your friends are true Hollywood players with a trivia contest. Guests can play either individually or as teams. Put together a bunch of questions and answers and start asking questions and keeping score. Questions can cover general movie trivia, or trivia about the Oscars, or both, and you can make the questions multiple choice to give everyone at least a shot at greatness. A fabulous source for all things movie-related is www.imbd.com, and you can always Google "Oscar trivia" to come up with tons of material. A few sample questions to get you started:

1. Who was the youngest actor ever to win an Oscar?

   A. Anna Paquin, *The Piano*

   B. Tatum O'Neal, *Paper Moon*

   C. Mary Badham, *To Kill a Mockingbird*

   D. Patty Duke, *The Miracle Worker*

Answer: B. Tatum O'Neal was a mere 10 years and 148 days old when she took home the little gold guy for her role in *Paper Moon*. Anna Paquin comes in second for her adorable role in *The Piano*. She was only 11 years and 248 days old when she won in 1993. Ugh, don't these statistics make you feel unaccomplished and old? Well, don't fear, there's still hope for you to jumpstart your acting career: Peggy Ashcroft is Oscar's oldest winner at 77 years old and 93 days, winning Best Actress for her role in *A Passage to India*.

2. Which actor was originally considered for Tom Hanks' role in *Forrest Gump*?

    A. Bill Murray
    B. Harrison Ford
    C. Jim Carrey
    D. Tom Cruise

Answer: A. Talk about a tough break for Murray; *Forrest Gump* won Hanks an Oscar for Best Actor and the film swept through the box office and awards ceremonies in 1994.

3. Which actor had the least screen time in the film that won him an Oscar for Best Actor?

    A. Dustin Hoffman in *Rain Man*
    B. Tom Hanks in *Philadelphia*
    C. Anthony Hopkins in *Silence of the Lambs*
    D. Michael Douglas in *Wall Street*

Answer: C. Anthony Hopkins is only onscreen for a total of 16 minutes in *Silence of the Lambs*, yet his creepy portrayal of Hannibal Lecter was enough for him to cinch the coveted award.

guess that line

Here's another entertaining movie game. Once again, people can play in teams or by themselves. Compile a selection of lines from favorite movies and have everyone guess which movie they came from. You can go with multiple choice to help out some of your less savvy guests. Samples for you:

1. "I picked the wrong week to stop sniffing glue."
   A. *Airplane*
   B. *The Breakfast Club*
   C. *Fast Times at Ridgemont High*
   D. *Animal House*

Answer: A. This great line comes to us from the high-brow drama *Airplane.*

2. "Snakes. I hate snakes."
   A. *Gorillas in the Mist*
   B. *Seven*
   C. *Crocodile Dundee*
   D. *Raiders of the Lost Ark*

Answer: D. Harrison Ford bemoans the snakes that fill every nook and cranny of the tomb he gets lowered into at the end of *Raiders of the Lost Ark.* Who knew that this hunk would be afraid of snakes?

3. "In case I forget to tell you later, I had a really good time tonight."
   A. *Lost in Translation*
   B. *Pretty Woman*
   C. *As Good As It Gets*
   D. *The Sound of Music*

Answer: B. One of the sexiest bitches around, Julia Roberts, says this charming line to Richard Gere in her breakthrough film *Pretty Woman.*

The Sexy Bitch's Party

Aim for a menu that honors Oscar's illustrious history. (Label all your food with names so guests make the culinary-cinematic connection.) If recipes are too much trouble, you can just get takeout *Lord of the* (onion) *Rings*, *Babe*'s *Revenge* (barbeque pork ribs, named for the 1995 Best Picture nominee that got squeezed out by movies starring humans, go figure), and *Chicago* pizza, after the 2002 winner for Best Picture. For dessert, set out a box of chocolates in honor of the big 1994 winner, *Forrest Gump*. Some Oscar-inspired recipes to try:

The Deliverance

Honor the Burt Reynolds classic about a guys' weekend in hillbilly country that goes horribly wrong (nominated for Best Picture in 1972) by having guests do a shot of whiskey. For the full effect, the drinker should be on all fours and squeal like a pig when finished.

The English Patient

Okay, so this is just a flaming Sambuca shot, but you can reinvent this old-standby as an Oscar fave by renaming it to commemorate the 1996 Best Picture winner starring Ralph Fiennes as a mysterious burn victim. Simply fill a shot glass with Sambuca and use a lighter to set the top of the liquid on fire. (You could also hold onto this title in case you burn any of your dishes for the evening beyond recognition. Simply stick it on a nice plate and label it "The English Patient.")

Braveheart Brew

This punch throws enough pow to make your hair stand on end like Mel Gibson's in the 1995 Best Picture winner. (Blue face paint is optional.)

1 liter Bacardi Limon
1 liter Triple Sec
1 liter Absolut Citron
2 liters fruit punch (in the frozen section of the grocery store)
Tons of ice cubes

Mix all ingredients together into a punch bowl and go nuts.

Titanic Salad

Throw in all of your favorite salad fixings: sunflower seeds, cukes, tomatoes—and don't forget a big hunk of iceberg lettuce in the middle of the salad bowl!

Lord of the Calamari Rings

This is a fried spicy calamari dish served with garlic aioli.

Calamari rings (amount depends on how many people you are
      inviting)
1 cup flour
2 Tbs. cayenne
1 Tbs. garlic powder
1 tsp. salt
1 tsp. white pepper
1 tsp. paprika
1 lemon (cut into wedges)
1/4 cup canola oil

Sauce:
1/2 cup mayo
2 tsp. lemon
1 Tbs. garlic
Dash salt, dash pepper, dash dill

Steps:

1. Mix together all dry ingredients in plastic bag.
2. Add calamari to flour mixture and shake in plastic bag.
3. Heat oil until just smoking, add calamari, and cook in batches until golden brown. (Don't cook it all at once or it won't brown!!)

Serve with lemon wedges and garlic aioli.

viva las vegas!

Do you want to get lucky? Need some glitz and glamour? Host a Vegas party and let the gambling begin! Set up several tables and have friends host various games, such as blackjack, poker, craps, the works. Decorate the "casino" with gaudy streamers and colored lights to bring the sin city closer. Serve old-school drinks like Manhattans, martinis, and sidecars and pretend you're swinging with the Brat Pack. You can play with high stakes or low stakes, whatever the crowd wants. Just stock up on dice, monopoly money, and gambling chips, and throw in some confetti and champagne to celebrate any high rollers. Depending on how spendy you feel, there are tons of different companies that rent casino equipment for parties, so the options are endless. And don't worry: what happens at your party, stays at your party.

Manhattan

2 oz. bourbon
1 oz. sweet vermouth
2 drops Angostura bitters
maraschino cherry

Serve on the rocks in a lowball glass, or mix with ice in a cocktail shaker and strain into martini glasses.

ski chalet soiree

There's nothing like a day of skiing to make you want to cozy up by the fire and suck down a few hot toddies. Host a party at your pad—doesn't have to be in Aspen—cut out little paper snowflakes, post some pics from some ski mags and some resort trail maps and you can bring the slopes anywhere. Tell friends to wear their ski wear and get ready for some *après* ski.

Aspen Apple Crisp

This cozy crowd pleaser takes minutes to assemble and can be modified to include all of the brown sugar that your sweet tooth craves.

8 cups sliced, pared apples (pick the variety that you prefer)
1 1/2 cups brown sugar
1 cup oats
1 cup flour
1 1/2 tsp. nutmeg
2/3 cup butter
1 tsp. vanilla

Steps:
1. Preheat oven to 375°F.
2. Lightly grease a 9x13 baking dish.
3. Mix all ingredients together except for the apples.
4. Put the apples on the bottom of the dish and cover with mixture.
5. Bake for 30 minutes.

scavenger hunt

Everyone loves a night to rummage around town and create mischief. Today scavenger hunts can be more fun than ever because you can take digital pictures of the shenanigans that cannot be transported back to home base. Your friends should get into groups of about four (or however many can fit in one car) and hit the road in search of their lists with a two- or three-hour time limit. Have fun with your local area and come up with some funny hunting items that capitalize on the unique features of your vicinity. Each person should pay $5 to play so that the there can be a kitty for the winning team. Set up a score sheet and make some pictures worth more than others depending on difficulty level.

Here are some possibilities for your scavenger hunt list:

- Find a house with the address 123 _____ Street
- Count the number of stools in a local bar (designate a specific bar)
- Get the car weighed at a truck weigh stop with all group members inside
- A group member holding a puppy under the age of 12 weeks old
- A group member standing by a street sign that is either their first or last name (this works best in an urban setting with tons of different streets)
- A local celebrity (designate someone specific) shaking hands with a group member
- A male group member trying on a bra at a local lingerie store (or buying some other feminine item at a drugstore)

luau

Sometimes we all need a little beach blanket bingo to spice up the dreary winter months. Instruct your friend to dress for a beach party. Turn up the heat and the tunes and get everyone swaying to the beat like palm trees. Okay, so maybe you're realizing that sunglasses will be essential not merely as a cute accessory but also to shield you from the blinding whiteness of everyone's exposed flesh. Have no fear: that's what bronzers and self-tanners are for. But rather than braving it in just a barely-there bikini, allow yourself to breathe more easily by sporting a sultry sarong. Break out your beach wear and get into the aloha spirit.

Fill the party space with a bunch of accessories, including inflatable beach toys, photos and posters of exotic tropical locales, and tiki lights. With this party, there is no such thing as too many palm fronds lying around—they're easier to clean up than carting in sand.

Serve mai tais and daiquiris and go with a pupu platter idea of many appetizers.

feeling sporty?

Do you have a team that is dear to your heart? If you don't, get one— because sporting events are a great excuse to party. Get your varsity squad of buddies together and get ready to roll. First of all, what event are you celebrating? Superbowl? World Series? Kentucky Derby? The Boston Marathon?

Whatever it is, start off with creating a snacks menu that reflects the host city and type of event. For example, if this is the World Series, and let's just say the Red Sox are in it (okay, okay, I'm from Boston, what can I say?), obviously you must combine baseball and Boston to create your shindig. So think about dishes that would represent the area: New England-style clam chowder, Boston brand beers, lobster? (Eeek, that's pretty spendy.)

Next, go with your type of event. Since my example is baseball, I would stock up on peanuts, popcorn, and hotdogs. You should also look for some quirky aspects to your team. For example, maybe I would concoct a big green cake and write "The Green Monster" on it to memorialize Fenway Park's special feature. For your basic sporting event, you'll want your culinary fare to reflect a sports bar menu, so think nachos, wings, and other indulgent foods. Fill a few bowls with chips, peanuts, and pretzels. You can also whip together a plate with submarine sandwich fixings, so that people can make their own sandwiches and snack around your other items. As all of the stadiums get redone, you can find anything from sushi to Ben and Jerry's ice cream in most of the newer stadiums, so you can find an excuse to serve just about anything you want.

Dress up in full team regalia. No, you don't have to shimmy your way into a pair of tight football pants, but you should be sporting a T-shirt that supports your team (duh!). You should also decorate your space with pics of the players. You can run different betting pools and even have a trivia contest about the team's history and its players, then award your winners with prizes.

When you've gotten people together for a sporting event, you need some sport. Yeah, you could run races around the block, but that would involve leaving your comfortable spot on the couch with a direct shot of the game on television, and no one wants to abandon a prime parking spot. So, your other option is getting your sport in the form of betting games.

dice – "41"

This game involves rolling six dice at a time, and you get six turns. You have two objectives: one is to "qualify" by rolling a four and a one. The other is to score the most points, thereby winning the kitty. Each time you roll, you must "keep" at least one of the numbers. For example, on your first turn you might roll one, two, two, three, five, and six. You would probably decide to keep the one and the six, and in your next turns you'd be hoping for a four and as many sixes as possible. Theoretically, you could hit the jackpot on your first roll and have a four, a one, and four sixes. If this is the case, you better be wearing some sexy lingerie because you're getting lucky tonight! But anyway, back to the game: assuming that you don't hit the jackpot instantly, you should continue trying to roll a four and a one. Once you have secured your four and one, try to score as many points as possible with the remaining four dice over your last few rolls. Twenty-four is the highest score. The kitty is usually a dollar a round per person, but feel free to get adventurous. Instead of a buck maybe you want to bet a round of body shots or perhaps a piece of revealing apparel.

You don't have to take the first four and one that you see. You may want to keep going for the sixes and bet you will roll a lowly one later in the game. Trust me: this game might sound simple, but when you get the gang hooting and hollering for the poor sucker hoping for a one on his last roll to qualify, you've just taken your good times up a couple of notches.

superbowl grid

This is a staple at all self-respecting Super Bowl Parties. A winner is crowned at the end of each quarter. Usually there is a small payout for the end of the first and third quarter, a slightly larger payout for half-time, and the biggest payout for the final score. It is much easier to show a diagram of the grid and then explain the details.

EAGLES

		4	5	2	0	1	3	9	7	8	6
P A T R I O T S	**2**	BigB	wank	Joe	Carl	SM	Lulu	Hunk	DH	Joe	Lulu
	3	SM	Hunk	Lulu	SM	Hunk	Kai	Joe	TT B	Carl	TTB
	6	Carl	Carl	SM	Lulu	wank	Joe	DH	wank	Joe	wank
	4	wank	Joe	wank	Slim	DH	SM	Joe	Lulu	SM	Hunk
	7	Hunk	SM	Kai	TT B	Joe	TT B	Lulu	DH	Kai	DH
	8	Joe	Kai	SM	wank	DH	Kai	SM	Joe	wank	TT
	9	Lulu	TT B	wank	TT B	SM	Hunk	Lulu	SM	Hunk	SB
	5	SM	Hunk	DH	DH	wank	SM	Joe	DH	TT B	Joe
	1	wank	DH	Lulu	SM	Hunk	wank	Carl	Kai	Lulu	DH
	0	Carl	Kai	SM	wank	SM	Lulu	Joe	TT B	DH	KL

Make a grid that's 11 boxes square, with one team across the top and the other team down the side. Tape it to the wall, preferably close to the TV, so that every time there is a score everyone will turn to the grid to see who is looking to win some dough. Before the game starts, partyers should buy squares on the grid, paying a dollar (or more, you choose) to write their name in whichever box they choose. Once all of the squares have been paid for and there are names in every box, write the numbers 0-9 on little slips of paper, put them in a hat, and pull them out one by one to fill in the row of numbers across the top. Then put them all back in again and do another drawing for the row of numbers along the side.

Don't fill the numbers in until AFTER everyone has chosen squares, otherwise you'll give an unfair advantage to the people who actually know something about football. This is an egalitarian game—it's about getting lucky, not about being a football expert.

Next, the game (I mean the one on television) starts. At the end of each quarter, the player whose box matches the game score wins! Now, even if you don't know much about football, you're probably wondering to yourself, what if they score more than 9 points during the game? Don't worry: for the purposes of the grid, we are only concerned with the last digit of each score. For example, if the first quarter ended Patriots 14, Eagles 10, Slim would win the jackpot for that quarter because the square he ended up with was Patriots 4 and the Eagles 0. (Remember you are taking the second digit of the score, so only the 4 and the 0 count.)

A word of advice: spell out the jackpot payout on the bottom of the grid. You're there to watch the game, eat the seven-layer dip, drink a few coldies, and have a good time—which doesn't include mediating midway though the game how much each quarterly winner gets. And don't require the winner to be present to claim the final jackpot. Also, this is a little sexy bitch flair, make the 6 and 9 automatic winning squares to add a little sizzle to the beginning of the game and to let everyone know what type of party they are in for. So DH would win (just make it a small prize, such as the cost of one square) for having Patriots 6 and Eagles 9, and SB would win for Eagles 6 and Patriots 9.

Submarine Sandwich Fixin's

Amounts will depend on the number of people you expect.

Sub sandwich rolls
Deli-sliced turkey
Deli-sliced roast beef
Deli-sliced pastrami
Deli-sliced salami
Deli-sliced Monterey Jack cheese
Deli-sliced cheddar cheese
Deli-sliced provolone
For garnishes: slice up some iceberg lettuce, tomatoes, and
   onions
Condiments should include: mustard, mayo, ketchup, gua-
   camole, and roasted red peppers

Spicy BBQ Chicken Wings

4-5 pounds of chicken wings and drumetts
Two 5 oz. bottles cayenne pepper sauce
8 Tbs. BBQ sauce
1 Tbs. garlic, chopped
3 tsp. pepper
1 tsp. salt
1 bottle blue cheese salad dressing
jicama or celery, sliced into sticks

Steps:
1. Mix together everything but the chicken, the blue cheese
   dressing, and the jicama/celery.

2. Pour mixture over chicken and marinate for a minimum of four hours.
3. Line two large baking dishes with foil, pour in chicken, and bake at 375°F for 45 minutes, basting with pan juices after 30 minutes.
4. Serve with slivered jicama or celery and blue cheese dressing.

Stuffed Grilled Peppers (Spicy!)

Large jalapeno peppers (number depends on the size of your party)
Several kinds of cheese including pepper jack, sharp cheddar, and your personal favorites (amounts will depend on the size of your party)

1. Slice jalapeno horizontally and fill with desired cheese.
2. Grill on BBQ until cheese is melted.
Serve as an easy accompaniment to grilled meats or as an appetizer with a cooling dip such as cilantro sour cream.

hosting a murder

If you have been watching too much "Law & Order," it's time to peel yourself off the couch and plan a murder party of your own. There are tons of companies and kits that will help you host one of these parties, or you can put together one of your own (although I can't lie, this can be a lot of work and requires scads of creativity). The main idea behind one of these shindigs is that you get everyone together for a dinner party, there's a murder (surprise!), everyone's a suspect, and everyone must solve the mystery to uncover the killer who lurks among you.

Here's what you need:

Support: Enlist the help of at least one other friend who can help you design the plot, play a supporting character, or simply manage the army of detectives once the mystery unfolds.

A setting: Your setting is what will dictate everything, including decoration, food, and costumes. Are you on a cruise ship? A college dorm? A tropical island? The Orient Express? Gilligan's Island? Hollywood party? A historical event?

A cast of characters: Design a bunch of characters for your guests and write up profiles. You can be very amusing here and give everyone intriguing professions, backgrounds, and idiosyncrasies. Don't be afraid to create complex relationships, such as affairs, lingering grudges, jealousies, and just plain bad blood between these characters, so that some interesting motives exist for foul play. Some typical archetypes for characters include: the gossip/busybody, the know-it-all, the lush, the jealous spouse, the eccentric millionaire, and the lowlife.

A plot: An easy way to figure out your plot is to lift one from the news, a television show, or a movie. Simply modify real events a little so the outcome won't be obvious to all of the players. It can be fun to modify a real-life crime so that everyone can weigh in on their own crazy theories of what happened.

Props: Yellow police tape, brass candlesticks, a dagger, a purse with ticket stubs inside and a note from a mystery man/woman…all of these are options for the props you will want to sprinkle throughout the party. Just know that your guests may get all kinds of crazy ideas into their heads and pursue theories that you never foresaw. That's okay, it's all part of the job of improvisation and unscripted fun.

Clues: Write down a series of clues that propel the plot of your story forward and hand them out to partyers as the evening unfolds. The clue can be an action (someone should do something) or background knowledge (a piece of titillating information that sheds some light on motive—or info that seems crucial but has no real bearing on the plot and is merely intended to distract the guests). Your guest should read the clue aloud, then everyone tries to figure out what has happened.

12 just us bitches: girls' night parties

There are few things more enjoyable than getting together your posse of girls for a sexy bitch night. Sure, men are great—but sometimes it's more fun to appreciate them from a distance (and it's definitely more fun to bitch about them that way)! You can create giggle-worthy decorations by taking a bunch of used cheesy bodice-ripper romance novels and gluing photos of your friends' faces over the faces of the heroines on the covers. If you are hosting a bachelorette party and you really want to roast the bride-to-be, use some sleazy magazines instead.

spa time

You and all the sexy bitches in your circle can spend an evening pampering yourselves with do-it-yourself manicures and other beauty treatments. Before the festivities begin, everyone can go out for an urban hike to get the blood flowing and some color in your cheeks. If a friend is a yoga goddess, have her take you through a few poses to relax and loosen up, or throw in a yoga video and try not to tear any muscles.

Serve some healthy smoothies, salads, and other tasty healthy treats, but keep it real by making sure you also have desserts that will blow everyone's diet out the window. You can drive your costs down by requiring each sexy bitch to show up with a bottle of her favorite nail polish color (or a beauty product of her choice).

Elise's Santorini Salad

2 heads butter lettuce, washed and separated
1 block feta cheese, crumbled
1 jar kalamata olives, drained
2 jars artichoke hearts, drained
1 cup sunflower seeds
1 large cucumber, diced
4 plum tomatoes, diced

Dressing:
1/2 cup olive oil
1 cup canola oil
1/2 cup red wine vinegar
1 clove garlic, minced
1 tsp. dried oregano
salt and pepper to taste

Steps:
1. Mix all of the salad ingredients together.
2. Whip up the dressing in a different bowl and pour on top of salad!

The Sexy Bitch's Party

The Healthy Bitch

1 1/2 cups chopped strawberries (fresh are fab, but go with
    frozen if it's all that's available
3/4 cup diced mango (once again, fresh mango is great, but the
    jars of pre-sliced mangoes make life easier)
3/4 cup guava nectar
1 frozen banana sliced into little chunks (use a sharp knife since
    it's frozen)

Mix it all in the blender and drink up! There are plenty of vitamins
packed in here, so swill it down.

Once everyone is feeling sufficiently healthy, blow it all out the
window with a couple of mudslides and fattening desserts.

Mudslides

1 oz. vodka
1 oz. Kahlua
1 oz. Bailey's Irish Cream

Fill a cocktail shaker with ice, add ingredients, and shake well
(see, you're still burning calories with a little exercise!). Strain
into a chilled glass.
Note: If you prefer frozen mudslides, blend all ingredients with
3-4 oz. of crushed ice until smooth.

clothing swap brunch

Are you suffering from a case of the wardrobe blues, yet so short on cash that you can't quite swing the idea of hitting your local Prada boutique with a clear conscience? Rather than hiding in your house out of sight of the much-feared fashion police, get the gals together for some brunch and tell them to bring some old clothes that still look good. This party works especially well for formal-wear that is still in great shape, so try to schedule this in early spring before the wedding circuit begins and you're stuck wearing the same dress to eighteen different weddings.

With this party, everyone gets to update their closet with some castoffs from some stylish friends. Just because you're sick of that swanky silver sequined number you've worn to the last three New Year's Eve parties, that doesn't mean someone else won't be ecstatic to turn it into her special outfit. This party is also a great way to unload some of those "super" bridesmaid dresses that your thoughtful friends have forced you to wear at their weddings. Or perhaps you've just had a baby and cannot quite wriggle into those size 2 suede pants anymore. A couple pairs of cute (and roomier) pants is just what you need to hold you over until you're back in fighting shape.

Make sure there's no odd woman out—either invite only guests who are about the same size, or have a sizeable contingent of every height and shape—so that everyone can end up a winner. This idea can also be modified to jewelry and other accessories, although I think I'd avoid a shoe swap—phew! If anyone suggests a boyfriend or husband swap, I think I'd nix the idea just so you don't end up in the uncomfortable position of having to make returns later.

Bellini Bender

This peachy drink makes champagne a classic breakfast beverage.

2 1/2 cups peach nectar
3 Tbs. fresh lemon juice
1 1/4 cups peach schnapps
5 medium peaches, sliced (frozen sliced will work if peaches aren't in season)
750 ml. bottle of dry champagne
crushed ice

Steps:
1. Combine everything in a large pitcher, except for the champagne.
2. Just before serving, add a bit of crushed ice and stir. Pour in champagne and serve.

Baked French Toast

loaf of French bread, cut into 8 or 10 slices about 1 1/2 inches thick
1 can apple pie filling
1 1/3 cup milk
7-9 eggs (use one less than the number of bread slices)
1/2 tsp. fresh grated nutmeg (or to taste)
1 tsp. cinnamon (or to taste)
1 tsp. vanilla (or to taste)
blueberries or strawberries (or both!)—1 small bag frozen or 1 box fresh

Steps:

1. Spray casserole dish with non-stick spray and line the bottom of the dish with apples.
2. Place bread slices on top.
3. Beat eggs, add milk and spices and then mix and pour over bread.
4. Let sit a few minutes to soak bottom, then turn over.
5. Cover and refrigerate overnight.
6. To cook, place berries between slices and bake at 350 °F for 40 minutes.
7. Separate bread slices with sharp knife if necessary.
8. Sprinkle with powdered sugar and serve with maple syrup.

babes in toyland

Partying and shopping at the same time—it's the ideal combo! Even better when you're shopping for sex toys. Get the gals together at your place to learn about new products and techniques that are guaranteed to bring loads of erotic pleasure. Lots of companies will send representatives to your house to educate your girlfriends (and sell them stuff in the process). Forget the mortification of learning about periods and STDs in your fifth-grade sex ed class, and stay open-minded about learning about the tricks of the trade through sexperts who can share all kinds of secret titillating moves with you in a totally professional environment.

Go online to choose a company for your party. Good Vibrations, a woman-founded company in San Francisco, is a good place to start your research. Check their website at www.goodvibes.com or just Google "sex toy party" to find companies with representatives in your area.

The catering for an event like this must be just right. Hopefully there is a good baker in your area that specializes in concocting erotic cakes. Who doesn't love a big penis cake? In addition, visit a local sex store or any gift store with a sense of humor for amusing adult party favors, such as penis water bottles, tits and penis pasta, or some other ridiculous thing.

This theme can obviously be adapted for a fun bachelorette party. If you're going this route, make sure it's a lingerie shower so things can get really kinky and fun. Also, many lingerie and sex stores will host bachelorette parties for scavenger hunts and other sexy party ideas, so get on the horn and start planning an erotic time!

Between the Sheets

Here's a drink to set the right tone.

1 oz. light rum
1 oz. brandy
1 oz. Cointreau
1 tsp. lemon juice

In a cocktail shaker filled with ice, combine all ingredients and shake. Strain the concoction into a highball glass filled with ice cubes.

pity party

Turn the concept of being dumped on its head! Have you or one of your friends recently ended a doozy of a relationship? Well, turn off *Steel Magnolias* and host a real pity party. Get the gals together and get ready to bitch about any dude who has ever wronged you. All of the grizzly details are welcome. Award prizes to: worst break up, biggest shit-head, most inconsiderate moment, worst potential mother-in-law, and best revenge story.

Everyone can bring odds and ends left over from exes and you can burn them as an exorcism in a bonfire. "I Never" is a good game for a get-together like this. Going around the circle, every player announces something that she has "never" done. If anyone else in the circle *has* done it, she must take a drink. You will learn all kinds of interesting things about the girls, such as who ended up with an ass-full of poison ivy after an al fresco tryst. Serve strong drinks, have some indulgent comfort foods on hand, and let the bitching begin. Warning: calorie counting is not allowed!

Hop, Skip, and Go Naked
(The Official Drink of Sexy Bitches Everywhere)

To truly feel good about yourself, the people around you, and the world, my sexy bitch posse and I recommend a special little drink known as Hop, Skip, and Go Naked. All you need is a cup or two of this treat, and I promise that you will be the most charming, fabulous, witty, and gorgeous bitch in town.

1 can frozen limeade
1 can frozen lemonade
2 liters lemon-lime soda
1/2 gallon vodka
A six-pack of pilsner-style beer. (Experiment and modify this
    ingredient to suit your taste. You may want to add more beer.
    Don't spend a lot on your beer; in this case, cheaper is better.)

Mix all of this together and do repeated taste tests. It's the taste test part of this drink-making process that is really fun.

The Sexy Bitch's Party

Ex-boyfriend Cookies

You can whip up a plate of sugar cookies using a gingerbread man cookie cutter. Provide some frosting, and you and your posse can decorate these cookies like men from your past. When you are done, you can bite their heads off and chew them to pieces. You can either use the easy recipe below or buy refrigerated tubes of sugar cookie dough. Just don't forget those pre-made dough rolls don't make that many cookies.

A gingerbread man-shaped cookie cutter
1 1/2 cups confectioner's sugar
1 cup butter-flavored shortening
1 egg
1 tsp. vanilla extract
1/2 tsp. almond extract
2 1/2 cups all-purpose flour
1 tsp. baking soda
1 tsp. cream of tartar

Steps:
1. Pre-heat oven to 350°F and lightly grease cookie sheets.
2. Mix the sugar, shortening, egg, vanilla, and almond extract until smooth and creamy.
3. Mix in flour, shortening, and cream of tartar.
4. Make several balls of dough and then roll them out into slabs that are no more than 1/4-inch thick.
5. Cut into slabs with cookie cutter and transport to cookie sheets with a spatula.
6. Bake for 8-10 minutes and enjoy your sweet revenge!

Ex-boyfriend Cookie Frosting

4 cups confectioner's sugar
1/2 cup shortening
5 Tbs. milk
1 tsp. vanilla extract
Food coloring

Steps:
1. In a large bowl, mix sugar and shortening together until smooth.
2. Gradually blend in milk and vanilla with hand blender until the mixture is stiff (usually about 5 minutes).
3. Separate portions of the frosting into bowls and add food coloring to get the palette that you want and start decorating.

Fancy Grilled Cheese Sandwiches

This is a delicious new take on an old classic comfort food staple.

A loaf of white sourdough bread
Brie cheese, blue cheese, and gorgonzola cheese
Figs, apples, and pears for slicing

Steps:
1. Butter 1 side of each slice of bread.
2. Create sandwiches with your selection of cheeses and fruit fillings.
3. Grill on stovetop with buttered sides of breads facing out until the bread is as dark as you desire.

classic sexy bitch movies

For a quieter evening, you and your gal pals may take solace in watching some other sexy bitches in action.

Gone with the Wind: There is no doubt that Scarlett O'Hara is the beginning of a long train of sexy bitches who mean business and don't take "no" for an answer.

Nine to Five: Three office gals (Jane Fonda, Dolly Parton, and Lily Tomlin) take revenge on their obnoxious, bigoted, sexist slob of a boss. You go, girls!

Thelma & Louise: Two frustrated housewives hit the road in search of adventure, alcohol, and orgasms. Brad Pitt's career started here when he bared his fabulous abs and gave Geena Davis something to holler about.

Erin Brockovich: Julia Roberts reprises her sexy bitch ways (remember *Pretty Woman*?) and plays a hot single mom bent on sticking it to a polluting California utility. This one is based on a true story.

Bridget Jones's Diary: Our favorite thirty-something singleton gets drunk, gets laid, and uses adorable British slang, like "snogging" and "shag." What's not to love?

Fatal Attraction: Although I don't recommend replicating Glen Close's revenge from when she gets jilted, this movie certainly can bring about a sense of satisfaction when you're mad at men.

Aliens: Sigourney Weaver's ass-kicking character, Ripley, will inspire you to save the planet. Or at least join a gym, maybe.

Kill Bill Volumes 1 and 2: The ultimate revenge fantasy—but don't try the yellow jumpsuit at home. Only Uma could make that look good.

bridal shower

If you're a true sexy bitch, the only type of bridal shower that you would ever consider hosting is a lingerie shower. We are not into fawning over the intricacies of china patterns, are we? No! Every new bride should have a collection of fabulous lingerie at her disposal so that she looks and feels fabulous even when she realizes that she is going to be sharing her bed with the same man for the rest of her life. Marriage is no time to let your guard down and succumb to girdles and cotton briefs like your granny would wear. Eeek! So, hook up your soon-to-be married sexy bitch with loads of racy little garments to keep her private life as interesting as it was before she took herself off the singles market.

Showers are often synonymous with shower games, and although these can be appallingly stupid, liven them up with some interesting twists…

bridal jeopardy

Yes, this is a take on the Alex Trebek classic (sans the old man), but the object is to quiz the audience with questions about the bride and her soon-to-be-husband. If mothers and mothers-in-law are present, you may want to tone down references to past sexual escapades. But wait a minute…this is a shower for sexy bitches so there shouldn't be anyone present who is easily shocked.

Before the shower, decide on about five or six categories for your game. Some suggestions are: Past Boyfriends, (insert bride's name) and (insert groom's name) History, Pet Peeves, Childhood, Most Embarrassing Moments, Accomplishments. Divide your guests into teams and have them choose their category. On a white board or poster assign values to each question, just like the screen is set up on the television show. The values can be drinks, pieces of candy, money, or whatever. For each correct answer, the team wins whatever is on the board. If they get their question wrong, the other team gets a shot at it. Play until all questions have been answered. The bride serves as a judge and she gets to join the winning team to savor their spoils.

don't say bride or wedding

This game is easy and can last through the whole shower. Anyone who says "bride" or "wedding" has to do a shot.

pass the box

This is a variation on musical chairs. Put an interesting and desirable item, such as a piece of lingerie or a bottle of wine, in a box and wrap it with many layers of wrapping paper. Everyone should sit in a circle and music should be played while everyone hands the box around. Whoever is running the game should have a stereo and they should turn it off intermittently. Whenever the music turns off, whoever is holding the box should unwrap one layer of gift wrap. Continue until the box is unwrapped. Whoever takes off the last layer wins whatever is in the box.

wedding dress designer

Divide guests into groups of three or four and give each group a roll or two of toilet paper. Using one of the team members as a model, each group should design a wedding dress using the toilet paper by wrapping up the model in it. Give the groups about 10 minutes or so to concoct their creations. The bride can choose the winner.

Giggly Bride Champagne Cocktail

1 quart of chilled lemonade
2 bottles of chilled champagne

Set out a pitcher of lemonade and the bottle of champagne.
Guests can mix the two to their liking.

baby shower

When one of your sexy bitch friends finds herself pregnant it is best not to lament the fact that her life is going to change forever in a way that seems incomprehensible to most fun-loving gals. Yes, suddenly there will be things like bedtimes and playgroups to worry about. While this may seem like the end of the sexy bitch lifestyle, it certainly doesn't have to be. I have many hot mama friends who know how to balance their adorable kids with a swinging social life. With this in mind, you want to make sure that you are setting up your friend to be a successful sexy bitch mama. When it comes to gifts for this gal, don't feel compelled to buy another set of baby booties. Most mothers will tell you that the amount of baby stuff that they have is ridiculous, so a gift that focuses on returning mama to her fabulous pre-stretched out self is always appreciated. By the way, tell the mother-to-be that she is getting a break: no one at the shower expects thank you notes. This sexy bitch has enough on her plate already!

Consider buying her a gift certificate to a spa or a restaurant, so that she can actually have a reason to leave her new precious bundle of joy. If you give a gift like this, make sure you accompany it with a babysitting coupon so that she really can enjoy her massage unencumbered by a wailing baby. The new mom may actually be reluctant to leave her little baby with a sexy bitch friend like you because she might know you best for antics that should not be witnessed by her innocent lamb; however, this problem is easily overcome. Simply tell her that you are also considering becoming a mom soon and you want some practice. Even if you would sooner shave your entire head than have a baby, she will eat this information right up because she so desperately hopes that it is true. And voila, you have just landed yourself a date with someone much, much too young for you. (Don't be afraid to use the TV as your babysitting assistant. Ignore all of the studies about how watching television leads kids inevitably to become vegetables or serial killers. Please! If you can mesmerize the little bugger with some TV, who cares what happens 10 years down the line.)

If you do find yourself suckered into hosting a baby shower, you will need to keep everyone entertained with some good gossip, strong drinks, and games. Here are a few games to get you started…

diaper disaster

Buy a bunch of different candy bars, melt them in the microwave, and put each of the melted remains in a different diaper. Pass them around to the guests and let them try to figure out which piece of candy is in each diaper. Guests can smell and taste the mess to help them figure out what each mess is. Gross but funny! Whoever can sniff out the most correct answers wins a prize (preferably some sort of birth control so you won't have to do this again anytime soon).

bottle bowling

Set up 10 baby bottles in a long hallway. Put them into a pyramid configuration like what you see at the bowling alley. Divide your guests into teams and have them use a tennis ball as a bowling ball. Predetermine how many rounds will be played and have each team shoot for the highest score. Have a prize for the winning team.

baby bingo

Before the gift-opening segment of the shower begins, have each guest make up a Bingo board. To do this, instruct each woman to make 3x3- or 4x4-square grid and write different things you need for a baby in each square. As the mother-to-be begins to open presents, have guests cross off any items on their board. The first one to get a line of three gifts in a straight row wins a prize.

Example:

Baby Hat	Pajamas	Blanket
Bottle	Books	Booties
Crib Bedding	Teddy Bear	Photo Album

Cry Baby Blues

Try this drink to put everyone (who's not pregnant) in the right mood.

4.5 oz. strawberry guava juice (located in the juice section of the grocery store)
1 oz. Blue Curacao
1 oz. Absolut vodka

Mix the ingredients together and serve with shaved ice.

Mama's Milkshake

And for the pregnant/nursing ones:

1 cup strawberries (fresh or frozen)
1 cup ice cream (strawberry or vanilla)
2 cups milk
(optional: chocolate syrup to taste)

Put the strawberries in the blender first and puree with a little milk. Then add the remaining ingredients and blend until smooth.

quiz: the ultimate party challenge

1. If you could only serve one food at a party, what would it be?

    A. guacamole

    B. cheese

    C. chocolate

    D. Gummi bears

Answer: C. This one's easy: we all need more chocolate in our lives. Note to self: must remember to call Senator and demand that chocolate be added to the food pyramid.

2. If you could invent something, which would be the most valuable to sexy bitch hostesses everywhere?

    A. Party Compass

    B. Hangover Cure

    C. Hootchie-Be-Gone Spray

    D. Insta-Cleaner Upper Potion

Answer: D. This is a tough one because all of these items are so desperately needed, but the top vote is to instantly be able to clean up your house, car, or office without lifting a perfectly manicured fingernail. Think of all of the entertaining you could do without having to clean up beforehand and afterward!

3. What is the best sexy bitch Halloween costume?

    A. Lorena Bobbit

    B. Queen Elizabeth I

    C. Princess Leia

    D. Madonna

The Sexy Bitch's Party

Answer: D. All of these options could be clever Halloween costumes, but Madonna really offers so many possibilities depending on the era that this theme could keep you in costumes forever.

4. A ski weekend falls through at the last minute. What do you do?
   A. Find a good book and curl up for a quiet weekend at home
   B. Keep your cute pink vest out and your wooly boots and plan a ski chalet soiree
   C. Call your grandmother and offer to do chores for her all weekend long
   D. Start calling friends to see what their plans are for the weekend

Answer: B. Yeah, yeah, reading is all well and good, and helping your grandma is noble, but get your partying act together and bring the ski weekend to you and your homies. Get out your scissors and start cutting out snowflakes to blanket the walls of your pad for a hot evening of chill *après* ski fun.

5. When planning a party, your first concern is:
   A. Determining a color scheme for the fete
   B. Creating the correct balance in your menu between starches, proteins, colors, and textures
   C. Scheduling a nap to catch some beauty sleep in the hours leading up to the big event
   D. Figuring out your seating chart

Answer: C. Forget making sure that you're not seating exes next to each other and making sure that all of your linens are the same shade of sage, toss it all and take a nap so you'll be ready to stay up all night!

6. Someone spills red wine all over your cream-colored rug. Yikes! What's a gal to do?

    A. Berate the spiller in front of everyone

    B. Grab the tonic water and start trying to get the stain out

    C. Go Jackson Pollock and have everyone spill their red wine on the rug and see if you can redesign it.

    D. Ignore it and deal with it the next morning

Answer: C. Yes, you should definitely try some tonic water first to see if they whole problem can be easily fixed, but if it's beyond hope consider it a sacrifice to the partying gods and start redecorating. Not only will everyone want your newest style rug, but everyone will admire your easygoing attitude.

7. An ex-boyfriend shows up at your birthday party WITH a hot new girlfriend and WITHOUT a present. What does a sexy bitch hostess do?

    A. Order them to leave

    B. Grab the nearest guy and start making out

    C. Be courteous and engage in idle chit chat with them both while hiding your fury

    D. Have a friend wrap up a gorgeous piece of jewelry and quickly write a card that says how much he misses you and open it in front of everyone.

Answer: D. Open the marvelous piece of hardware and relish the oooohs and aaaahs around you while paying special attention to the look of fury on his current girlfriend's face. Shake your head confidently and remind him that it's over and say normally you couldn't possibly accept such a luxurious gift, but you'll hold on to this one as a token of friendship.

The Sexy Bitch's Party

8. What should every sexy bitch have in her hostessing toolkit?

    A. a barbeque

    B. a waffle iron

    C. massive quantities of gelatin and a baby pool

    D. margarita salt

Answer: A. While all of these items can contribute to a good party, a barbeque is really essential. First of all, it allows you to whip up great food in bulk with little hassle. Second of all, men love barbeques and you will be surrounded by a group of worshippers as you commandeer this wonderful cooking tool.

9. What's the best way to spread the word about a last-minute party?

    A. carrier pigeons

    B. email

    C. start calling everyone's cell phone

    D. have someone else send emails and call everyone

Answer: D. C'mon: you must work smart and delegate if you want to be a real sexy bitch hostess. Calling all of your peeps will take eons, so get some of your friends to help you out to spread the word while you assemble your party vision.

10. If a fellow sexy bitch is going through a tough time, what is the best way to help?

    A. send her a card

    B. send a hit-man out on the person who is responsible for her woes

    C. throw her one of your world-famous parties

    D. take her shopping

QUIZ: THE ULTIMATE PARTY CHALLENGE

Answer: C. Although D is a close second, you really need to throw this gal a bender with plenty of stiff drinks, great tunes, and yummy men. Hmmm, perhaps take her shopping that afternoon and make it a double whammy. She may declare that she is not up for a party, but crown her royalty for the day or celebrate her birthday (who cares if it is eight months from now?) or choose a theme that is sure to brighten her up. After all, sexy bitches have to stick together and take care of one another. Rally on!

other books by ulysses press

The Sexy Bitch's Book of Doing It, Getting It and Giving It
Flic Everett, $9.95

Dishes the dirty truth on everything from foreplay and oral sex to sex toys and fantasy games.

The Sexy Bitch's Book of Finding Him, Doing Him and Dating Him
Siobhan Kelly, $9.95

If you're ready to go out and get what you want, this book offers invaluable tips on everything from clothes and chat topics to the sexiest ways to undress and the most unforgettable things to do once you're naked.

So You Wanna be a Sexy Bitch: Raise Your Game from Overlooked Nice Girl to Skilled Chick Everyone Wants to Get With
Flic Everett, $9.95

A road map to raising a woman's self image in the area of life where it matters most: sex.

Naughty Girls' Night In
Shana Duthie and Stacey Jewell, $14.95

From enjoying a night of fun with girlfriends to starting a profitable home business, this book describes everything you need to know about in-home adult sex toy parties.

Lose That Loser and Find the Right Guy: Stop Falling for Mr. Unavailable, Mr. Unreliable, Mr. Bad Boy, Mr. Needy, Mr. Married Man, and Mr. Sex Maniac
Jane Matthews, $12.95

This book helps a woman identify the wrong type of man, change negative dating habits, and build a relationship that is right for her

A Girl's Guide to Money
Laura Brady, $12.95

Seriously helpful financial advice communicated in a full-color, fun, girl-friendly style so young women can become financially savvy.

The Sexual Revolution 2.0: Getting Connected, Upgrading Your Sex Life, and Finding True Love—or at Least a Dinner Date—in the Internet Age
Regina Lynn, $14.95

Author Regina Lynn doesn't fear technology, she passionately embraces it. *The Sexual Revolution 2.0* is her personal roadmap for navigating the new sex/tech revolution.

The Wild Guide to Sex and Loving
Siobhan Kelly, $16.95

Packed with practical, frank and sometimes downright dirty tips on how to hone your bedroom skills, this handbook tells you everything you need to know to unlock the secrets of truly tantalizing sensual play.

To order these books call 800-377-2542 or 510-601-8301, fax 510-601-8307, e-mail ulysses@ulyssespress.com, or write to Ulysses Press, P.O. Box 3440, Berkeley, CA 94703. All retail orders are shipped free of charge. California residents must include sales tax. Allow two to three weeks for delivery.

about the author

LULU DAVIDSON lives and parties in the Pacific Northwest with her husband, Sassy Bastard, and Laci, the Party Pup. She teaches writing and is always seeking to blend business with pleasure. Her upcoming projects include working with Congress to create "National Wear Your Feather Boa to Work Day." Viva la sexy bitch!

acknowledgments

Thank-yous must be extended to a few special sexy bitches who helped me put this book together. Special thanks go to my super sister-in-law Kelly for all of her recipes, and to the rest of my family for their support. Colleen and Nancy can always be relied on for great party ideas, so I owe you both! Kristin, Michele, Courtney, and Becky also deserve special recognition for keeping me going when I was dragging. And last, but not least, the biggest thanks goes to David for keeping me sexy and not just a bitch. Now . . . let's celebrate!